EARLY YEARS
ACTIVITY CHEST

Early reading

British Library Cataloguing-in-Publication Data
A catalogue record for this book is available from the British Library.

ISBN 0 439 01729 7

ACKNOWLEDGEMENTS

The publishers gratefully acknowledge permission to reproduce the following copyright material:

Jillian Harker for 'Billy Goats Gruff'; 'Cats, cars and trains'; 'All dressed up' © 2000, Jillian Harker; Celia Warren for 'Building bridges'; 'The hamster and the hiccups' © 2000, Celia Warren. All previously unpublished.

Every effort has been made to trace copyright holders and the publishers apologize for any inadvertent omissions.

AUTHOR
Lorraine Gale

EDITOR
Susan Howard

ASSISTANT EDITOR
Lesley Sudlow

SERIES DESIGNER
Lynne Joesbury

DESIGNER
Paul Cheshire

ILLUSTRATIONS
Angie Sage

COVER PHOTOGRAPH
Fiona Pragoff

Designed using Adobe Pagemaker
Published by Scholastic Ltd, Villiers House,
Clarendon Avenue, Leamington Spa, Warwickshire CV32 5PR

Vist our website at www.scholastic.co.uk

1 2 3 4 5 6 7 8 9 0   0 1 2 3 4 5 6 7 8 9

CONTENTS

CONTENTS

Introduction

The ability to read is essential in today's literate society. There are few areas of our lives that do not involve reading, whether it is following the cooking instructions on a packet, checking the dosage on a medicine bottle or deciding which television programme to watch. However, we do not just read for information. We read to learn about the world in which we live, to get new ideas and to explore other's opinions. It is also frequently a pleasurable and enjoyable activity.

Reading is a complex skill. A reader needs to be able to recognize written letters and know their corresponding sounds, including those for combinations of vowels and consonants. They also need to know how they can make educated guesses at previously unknown words by looking for contextual and grammatical clues in the pictures and the surrounding words and sentences. As a child becomes more experienced at reading, he or she also needs to understand the mechanics of a book – how to use an index page and find pages by their numbers.

Reading is an active, problem-solving process, which depends on the individual reader's ability to predict, based upon their prior knowledge and experience. Because of this, when planning children's reading activities, we need to be aware of the knowledge and experiences that each child has of reading – including watching how an individual handles a book, checking the child's letter recognition, their phonic awareness, and discovering how the child views the act of reading in general.

There is no specific method for teaching children to read. Most educators agree that the best way to help children to read is to teach them as many ways as possible to read a word – where it is in the sentence, what its initial is and so on. This should be done through the use of a wide range of books and written materials so that the learning is in a meaningful context. Ideally, there should be a mix of formal teaching such as flashcards, and informal teaching such as answering a child when they ask a question about something that they have read.

To make children more aware of books and print and to help them realize that books and reading are valued, they need to see it in their environment and to see others reading. To create the right environment, label as many things as possible around your room such as coat hooks, displays of work and resources. Provide lots of good-quality books and encourage the children to handle them carefully but enthusiastically and to tidy them away when they have finished with them. Let the children see you reading letters from parents, books or messages and try to plan time when you can share a book with an individual or a group of children. If possible, create a 'reading corner' in an area of your room. Arrange books in open boxes or on open shelves, and add rugs, cushions and comfy chairs so that the children feel inspired to spend time investigating the books in comfort. You could also consider adding pot plants, small table lamps with light shades and a cassette recorder with headphones for listening to taped recordings of books.

The aim of the book

The main aim of this book is to provide activities that can help children to become competent readers. The book contains sixty activities. Each main activity is designed to be used with an 'average' four-year-old. However, as children differ in their needs, skills, abilities and knowledge, suggestions to simplify the main activity for younger or less able children ('Support') and ideas to extend the work for more competent readers ('Extension') are also included for each activity.

The book is closely linked to the Early Learning Goals (Qualifications and Curriculum Authority). There are six chapters – one chapter for each curriculum area mentioned in the Early Learning Goals. At the beginning of each activity there is a 'Learning objectives' section that outlines the specific skills, concepts, knowledge and attitudes that the children will be learning as they complete the activity. There are two learning objectives for each activity: the first objective refers to the area of learning covered by the chapter in which the activity occurs; the second objective details the knowledge and understanding of reading that the activity aims to teach. The main areas of reading that are covered are: phonic awareness; bibliographic awareness; grammatical knowledge; awareness of the purpose of writing and pictures in a book.

The activities

All of the activities in this book are designed to be short stand-alone time fillers. Most take only five to fifteen minutes. Each activity is presented on a separate page and includes the learning objectives, a list of resources needed, any necessary preparation, step-by-step instructions on how to carry out the activity, ways to simplify or extend the activity, ideas to promote home links with parents and carers and, for many activities, suggestions of ways to adapt the activity to promote multicultural learning.

Each activity includes a suggested group size. Sometimes, a specific number is given, such as 'four to six children'. Other activities suggest groups of 'any size'. These should, ideally, include no more than ten children. These are only recommendations, and could easily be adapted depending on the needs of your children, the adult to child ratio, and the resources available.

Photocopiable sheets

This book includes twelve photocopiable sheets that support some of the activities. Specific details on the number of photocopies needed, whether you need one sheet per child or just one for the group to share, are listed in the relevant activities. To prolong the life of the photocopies, it may be advisable to stick them onto thick card and cover them with plastic covering film.

Resources

All of the resources listed for the activities should be readily available in most early years settings. Consideration has been given to the fact that computer hardware and software is quickly outdated, and therefore none of the activities specifically require the use of computers.

Several of the activities suggest books to use during the activity. Most of these books are only recommendations, especially the non-fiction books or traditional tales such as 'Goldilocks and the Three Bears'. If you do not have a copy of the listed book, you could substitute a suitable book of your own.

A handful of the activities do require a specific book. If you do not have a copy of the book, try asking colleagues whether they have a copy that they could lend you, or alternatively, try your local library.

The types of books that you provide for the children are very important. Ideally, there will be good range of both fiction and non-fiction books, including traditional and modern tales, poems, rhymes and songs. Check the text in each book to make sure that it is appropriate for the age of your children. The children should know and understand most of the words in a book. Also, look for clear pictures that enhance the text and improve the reader's understanding of the writing. It also helps if the books that you choose are ones that you like, as this will translate into enthusiasm for the books that the children can see. If possible, try to include several 'big' books. These are ideal, due to their size, for group work and shared reading. Read to the children regularly, and vary the time that you read the story. It does not have to be at the end of the session just before everyone goes home.

When you are reading with children, make sure that everyone is sitting comfortably. This is important whether it is one child reading to you, or you are reading to a large group of children. Read any unfamiliar books through at least once before reading them to the children. This gives you a chance to notice any words that the children might not know, or to plan spaces where you could stop and talk to the children about the events in the book, or think about specific grammar points such as why some words are in bold text. When reading, keep your voice loud enough so that everyone listening can hear, even when you need to whisper, pausing at the punctuation marks. Try to use different voices for each character and to think about the speed of your reading and the pitch and intonation of your voice.

Home links

Each activity includes a short section which explains how the main activity could be adapted so that children and carers can try it together at home, or alternatively, suggests how the carers can extend and support the learning that the children have already done. The term 'carers' has been used throughout the book to refer to parents, foster parents and other friends or relatives who may look after the child once they return home.

Multicultural links

Many of the activities in the book suggest ways that the activities can be altered or adapted to help the children learn more about other cultures. Try to find examples of books that show positive images of people and traditions from other cultures and do not reinforce gender stereotyping.

CHAPTER 1

Personal, social and emotional development

The activities in this chapter will help children to develop an awareness of themselves and others and use their developing skills to interact with confidence. Ideas include reading and writing simple labels, classifying different texts and using a favourite story to think about what is right and what is wrong

GROUP SIZE
Any size.

TIMING
Ten to 20 minutes.

HOME LINKS
Make a sheet for the children to take home containing common words such as 'fridge', 'table' and 'door'. Draw boxes around each word and ask carers to help their children to cut out the words and attach them to the appropriate objects.

WHERE DOES THIS GO?

Learning objectives
To treat property with care and concern; to write labels and read a range of familiar and common words.

What you need
White card; scissors; black marker pen; large sheet of white paper.

Preparation
Cut the white card into appropriately-shaped labels for a variety of your resources. For example, you might cut triangular-shaped or circular-shaped labels for mathematical resources and pencil-shaped labels for art materials. You could also link labels to topics and themes in role-play areas. For example, a 'garden centre' might have labels shaped like a six-petalled flower, and name labels during a topic on transport could be cut into the shape of cars or trains.

What to do
Explain to the group that you would like to make some labels with the names of things on, for example 'brushes', 'calculators' and 'plastic bricks'. Ask the children for suggestions of objects that could be labelled and write their ideas down on the large sheet of paper.

Write the labels by acting as a scribe, or asking the children to copy-write each object name onto a pre-cut label. Some of the labels could include quantities such as '10 rulers' or '6 brushes'. You could also make labels that show the number of children that can carry out an activity at a time, for example, '4 can paint a picture' or '2 can write a letter'. Invite the children to help you display the labels around the room. When it is time to tidy away, ask the children to look for the appropriate labels.

Support
Make the labels slightly larger. Draw a picture of the item alongside the name on the label or stick on a picture of it cut from a magazine (old educational supplies catalogues are ideal for sources).

Extension
Give each child a written label. Ask them to read the label and find the correct place in your setting to display it. Alternatively, ask everyone to write a label independently while thinking about the letter sounds. Use simple dictionaries to help with spellings.

FIND ME A BOOK

Learning objectives

To work as part of a group, taking turns and sharing fairly; to read a range of familiar and common words and to sort books according to classification.

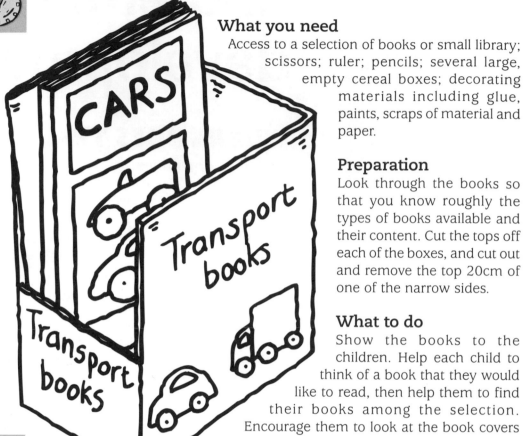

What you need

Access to a selection of books or small library; scissors; ruler; pencils; several large, empty cereal boxes; decorating materials including glue, paints, scraps of material and paper.

Preparation

Look through the books so that you know roughly the types of books available and their content. Cut the tops off each of the boxes, and cut out and remove the top 20cm of one of the narrow sides.

What to do

Show the books to the children. Help each child to think of a book that they would like to read, then help them to find their books among the selection. Encourage them to look at the book covers for clues about the contents. Ask questions such as, 'Can you find another *Spot* book by Eric Hill?' or 'Can you find a book with cars on its cover?'.

Explain to the children that sometimes we need to group books so that we can find them easily. Show them how most of the books will fit into the cut-down cereal boxes. Ask the children for suggestions of ways in which the books could be sorted – perhaps by subject (the transport books together), or by author (all the Dahl books).

Once the children have decided on their classification system, encourage them to work together, sharing resources to decorate the outside of the boxes and write on the contents of each box. When the glue or paint has dried, ask the children to help you fill the boxes with the relevant book titles. Encourage them to put the books back in the correct boxes when they have finished with them. If possible, take the children to a library or bookshop to look at how the books are organized there.

Support

Provide a small selection of books to classify and keep the categories broad, for example, 'story-books' and 'information books'.

Extension

Give older children a wider selection of books, and begin to introduce the alphabet as a filing system.

GROUP SIZE
Any size.

TIMING
Five to ten minutes.

HOME LINKS
Tell carers about the theme of the book display, and ask if they have any books on that subject that they could lend to the group. Ask them to choose a non-fiction book, such as a recipe book, and to look through it with their children.

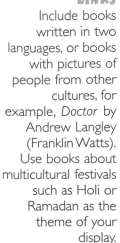

MULTICULTURAL LINKS
Include books written in two languages, or books with pictures of people from other cultures, for example, *Doctor* by Andrew Langley (Franklin Watts). Use books about multicultural festivals such as Holi or Ramadan as the theme of your display.

ALL ABOUT DOCTORS

Learning objectives
To initiate ideas and speak in a familiar group; to develop understanding about how information can be found in non-fiction books, and to learn vocabulary about books and print.

What you need
Variety of books connected to one theme, such as doctors.

Preparation
Display the books with suitable labels. These could include an explanation of the theme of the books and captions describing the books, for example, 'This book has pictures of hospitals', or challenges, for example, 'Can you find a book about nurses?'. If the books are linked to a topic that the children are currently learning about, display the books at the start of the topic so that they can use the books for their work.

What to do
Show the books to the children and explain their theme. Talk with the group about the types of books displayed – are they story-books, information books, or a mixture of both? Choose a simple non-fiction book with short contents and index pages. Ask the group what they would like to know about doctors, for example, 'Do doctors drive ambulances?'. Explain that if we know roughly what we want to find out we can use the contents page. If we have a question, and know how one of the important words (such as ambulance) is spelled, we can use an index page. Demonstrate by  using the contents and index pages to answer several of the children's questions. Encourage the children to practise finding information using both the contents and index pages. Invite the children to help you compile the display by telling them the theme in advance so that they can try to find suitable books to add to it.

Support
Introduce only a contents page, working with groups of four to six children and multiple copies of one book.

Extension
Choose books with more challenging text, and longer contents and index pages. Explain to the children how glossaries are used.

GROUP SIZE
Any size.

TIMING
Ten minutes (or longer if desired).

HOME LINKS
Give the children a short version of 'Goldilocks and the Three Bears' to take home to read with their carers.

MULTICULTURAL LINKS
Read multicultural books such as *That New Dress* by Malorie Blackman (Simon & Schuster Young Books) to the group and let the children take on the roles of the different characters in the books.

LET'S ASK QUESTIONS

Learning objectives

To develop an understanding about what is right, what is wrong and why; to learn about elements of stories including the main character and sequence of events.

What you need

A prop to identify you as 'Goldilocks', for example a wig or a large bowl or spoon; story of 'Goldilocks and the Three Bears' (Traditional).

Preparation

Read through 'Goldilocks and the Three Bears' so that you have a good knowledge of the events of the story and their sequence. Try to predict some questions that the children might ask about the story and think of reasons why Goldilocks may have acted the way she did. For example, 'Why did she eat the porridge?', 'Was she hungry?'.

What to do

Read the story of 'Goldilocks and the Three Bears' to the group so that the children are familiar with it. Explain that you are going to pretend to be Goldilocks. Show the children your prop and tell them that when you pick it up, you will pretend to be Goldilocks, but when you put it down you are yourself again. When you are Goldilocks, the children can ask you any questions about Goldilocks that they wish to. To help them, you could begin your time in the role of Goldilocks by explaining how you found the cottage, your reasons for going inside it and why you ate the porridge. Now invite the children to ask you some questions. Try to answer them as you think Goldilocks might have. If necessary, prompt by saying, 'Let me tell you why I...'. You could also take on the roles of other characters from the story. How would Baby Bear feel when he saw that his chair was broken? Would Daddy Bear like his bed being slept in?

Support

Without taking on the role of Goldilocks, use the book as a stimulus to ask the children questions such as, 'Why did Goldilocks eat the porridge?', 'Do you think that Goldilocks was scared when the bears came home?'.

Extension

Let the children take turns to be Goldilocks.

GROUP SIZE
Any size.

TIMING
Up to five minutes.

HOME LINKS
Put the cards on a large table near the door before each session. Ask carers to help their children find their names when they arrive and put them in the 'I'm here' box.

MULTICULTURAL LINKS
Make a poster to display on or near the door with 'Welcome' written in a variety of languages.

WHO'S HERE TODAY?

Learning objectives
To select and use activities and resources independently; to read own name and make comparisons with other names.

What you need
Card; scissors; marker pen; a box.

Preparation
Cut out individual name cards for the children and write on both their first names and family names. Prepare the box by writing 'I'm here' on it. Both the box and cards could be themed, perhaps to fit in with a topic. For example, for a topic on 'Growing', the box could be a plant pot, and the cards shaped like flowers, or during work on 'Myself', the box might be a wardrobe, and the cards shaped like T-shirts.

What to do
Explain that everyone has a card with their name on. Hold the cards up one by one for the children to try to recognize their names. Help the children to read the words by concentrating on the initial letters and the shape of the word. Spread the words on a large table or the floor and ask the children, in small groups of three or four, to find their names and put them in the box marked 'I'm here'.

Before the start of a subsequent session, you could display the name cards around the room next to the activities that you would like the children to go to. You could also encourage the children to send letters to each other, by making a post-box for each child, and putting their name on the front of it.

Support
Make sure the name cards are fairly large. To help identification, add photographs of the children or ask each child to draw a picture of themselves next to their names. If none of the children have the same first names, write just these on the name cards.

Extension
Instead of writing the children's full names, write 'Miss Philips', or each child's initials. Choose one child every session to check who is present in the group and to put the appropriate cards for all those in the room in the 'I'm here' box.

SHH! WE'RE READING!

Learning objectives

To develop independence in selecting resources and improve concentration; to select and read independently a variety of familiar and unfamiliar texts.

What you need

Selection of books; clock or watch.

Preparation

Find yourself an adult book to read during the quiet time.

What to do

Tell the children that when you have finished speaking, you would like everyone to choose a book to look at and read quietly for a few minutes. You may need to remind the children that quiet reading does not mean talking to a friend or walking around the room! Let the children choose the books that they want, and then either sit down at a table or on a carpeted area with them.

Once everyone is settled, begin to read your own book too. Initially, keep the quiet time to no more than five minutes. At the end of the allocated time, ask the children to put their books away tidily. Once they have put their books away, encourage them to give short book reviews to the rest of the group, explaining the title and author of the book and whether or not they enjoyed reading it. Alternatively, give pairs of children identical books to read, and, at the end of the quiet time, ask them talk with each other about the book that they have just read.

Support

Keep the quiet time to only two or three minutes and increase it gradually. Let younger children, who cannot read well, choose two or three books each to look at during the quiet time.

Extension

Increase the quiet time to ten or 15 minutes. When the reading time has finished, ask some of the children in the group to talk about the books that they have been reading and say whether or not they liked them. Some of the children may have chosen a book that they have not read before by using the cover and pictures as clues to the content of the book. If this was the case, ask the children if the book was everything that they expected it to be?

GROUP SIZE
Any size.

TIMING
Five to 20 minutes
(dependent on the
length of the book).

HOME LINKS
Provide carers with
guidelines on how
to read with their
children, or a list of
recommended
books. The Book
Trust publishes a
yearly guide to the
best books of the
year called *100 Best
Books*. Contact
Book Trust, Book
House,
45 East Hill, London
SW18 2QZ.
Tel: 0208-516 2977.

**MULTICULTURAL
LINKS**
Read multicultural
books such as
Greedy Zebra by
Mwenye Hadithi
(Hodder and
Stoughton) or
Jamela's Dress by
Niki Daly (Frances
Lincoln).

READ WITH ME!

Learning objectives

To maintain attention, concentrate and sit quietly; to enjoy books, learn book-related vocabulary and answer questions about where, why and how.

What you need

A picture book with text appropriate to the age of the children. Big books such as *This is the Bear* by Sarah Hayes and Helen Craig (Walker Books) are ideal.

Preparation

Read through the book beforehand so that you are familiar with the story.

What to do

Ask the children to sit down so that they are all facing you. Introduce the book by telling the children the title of the book and the name(s) of the author and illustrator. Hold the book so that all the children can see the pictures, and you can read the text comfortably. When reading the story to the children, pause briefly at the punctuation marks and try not to read too quickly. Use different voices for each character and try to put expression into your voice.

Read a wide variety of books to the group including poems, non-fiction books and traditional tales. When you have finished reading to the children, look at the pictures together or discuss whether or not the children liked the book.

Once the children are used to you reading books aloud, try occasionally stopping reading at a convenient point in the story and asking the children to predict what happens next. Choose a book that has big pictures and few words such as *Not Now, Bernard* by David McKee (Anderson Press).

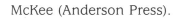

Support

Use a book that has large pictures and simple text including many words that the children can understand. The children will be able to relate more easily to books that are set in familiar places such as homes, shops and parks.

Extension

Choose a book for the children that has slightly harder text, a wider variety of characters or a more fantastical theme, for example, a fairy-tale such as 'Jack and the Beanstalk' or 'Rumpelstiltskin'.

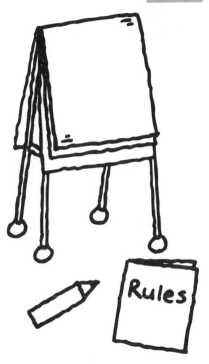

OUR LIST OF RULES

Learning objectives

To manage own personal hygiene and to understand the need to have agreed clues and codes of behaviour; to recognize familiar words and symbols and to know that words can be written down to be read again.

What you need

Flip chart or large sheet of paper and easel; felt-tipped pens; sheets of white A4 card or paper; examples of rules such as *The Highway Code* (HMSO), fire exit procedures or game rules.

Preparation

Collect resources and find examples of rules.

What to do

Sit the children down so that they can all see the easel and paper or flip chart. Show the children the examples of rules that you found, then discuss together some of the rules at your setting, such as 'Walk around the room' or 'Put rubbish in the bin'. Encourage the children to think of other rules. As the children make their suggestions, write their ideas down on the paper or flip chart. Try to keep the rules as positive as possible and avoid negative words such as 'don't' or 'no'. You could also use this opportunity to reinforce letter formation or simple punctuation using capitals and full stops.

Once you have a short list of rules, copy each one out onto a sheet of card or paper. Let the children decide where the rules should be displayed. Encourage the children to read the signs to each other and to you, especially if they need to be reminded of any of the rules. If you prefer, the rules could be compiled into a book rather than being positioned around the room. Alternatively, the children could make a book of 'silly rules' such as, 'Always wear a green hat outside' or 'Always stand on one leg on the carpet'.

Support

Write the rules in the fewest words possible, ideally using words that the children can already read. Ask the children to draw suitable illustrations for each rule. Encourage the children to read the rules by looking at the whole of the sentence and using the pictures for clues.

Extension

Ask each child to write down a rule that they can read to the other children in the group.

GROUP SIZE
Any size.

TIMING
Ten to 15 minutes initially; two or three minutes to update the tree.

THE APPLE TREE

Learning objectives
To consider the consequences of their words and actions for themselves and others; to read and compare names and familiar words.

What you need
Large piece of corrugated card or dark brown card; large piece of green paper; red paper; marker pen; scissors; staple gun or pins; Blu-Tack.

Preparation
Cut the brown card or corrugated card into the shape of a large tree trunk. Staple or pin to the wall at child height. Cut the foliage for the tree from the large sheet of green paper and attach to the wall at the top of the trunk. Cut the red paper into apple shapes.

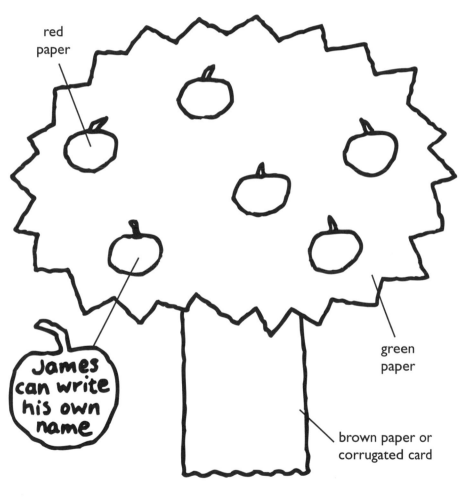

red paper

green paper

James can write his own name

brown paper or corrugated card

What to do
Show the children the tree and the apples. Explain to the group that on each apple you are going to write something good about someone and that person's name. For example, 'Charlotte can fasten her coat', 'James can write his name' or 'Tyrone helped Sasha when she fell over'. Ask the children to suggest things that could be written about them.

Write out an apple for every child and stick them to the tree with Blu-Tack.

Update the tree regularly, and try to find something to praise everyone for. Encourage the children to look for new apples on the tree, to find their name and read what has been written on their apple. Make individual books for each child with the title 'I can...'. When apples are removed from the tree, they can be glued into the relevant child's book with a date when the apple was written.

HOME LINKS
Tell carers about the apple tree and ask them to notify you of anything special that their children have achieved such as swimming awards, or any new skills that they have learned.

Support
Make larger apples. Write each apple with the child and ask the child to draw a picture to accompany the sentence.

Extension
Ask the children to write their own apples. Encourage them to sound out the words as they write them. Use simple dictionaries to check spellings that the children are unsure of. Alternatively, the children could write apples about each other, such as 'Thank you Kyle for helping me to find my hat'.

GROUP SIZE
Two to four children.

TIMING
Five to ten minutes.

HOME LINKS
Give the children copies of the baseboard and rules so that they can play the game at home with their carers. Give each child a letter and ask them, with the help of their carer, to find as many objects as possible around the home that begin with that letter.

MULTICULTURAL LINKS
Replace the snakes and ladders with objects considered lucky and unlucky by other cultures. For example, elephants, which are considered lucky for Hindus, and the face of Ravana, which Hindus consider to be unlucky.

ALPHABET GAME

Learning objectives
To work as part of a group and take turns; to read individual letters of the alphabet and know their corresponding sounds.

What you need
A copy of the photocopiable sheet on page 73; dice; variety of coloured counters (one for each player).

What to do
Initially, the children may need some adult help. Ask each child to choose a counter. Put all the counters on the 'Start' square. Each player throws the dice and the player who rolls the highest number goes first. On each player's turn, they throw the dice and move their counter a number of squares equal to the number shown on the dice. If the player lands on the bottom of a ladder, they can move their counter up to the top of it. However, if they land on a snake's head, the player must move down the snake until they reach its tail. When the player has finished moving, they say aloud the letter that they have landed on. The winner is the first player to land on the 'Finish' square.

Support
To make the game easier and shorter, omit the rules about the snakes and ladders. The children just move normally around the board passing from square to square as dictated by the dice roll and saying the letter that they land on.

Extension
Whenever a letter is landed on, each player must try to think of a different word beginning with that letter. Alternatively, have a collection of objects with the same initials as those on the baseboard. Whenever the children land on a letter, ask them to find an object in the collection that has an initial sound that matches it.

CHAPTER 2

Communication, language and literacy

In this chapter, children can explore and experiment with a wide variety of sounds, words and texts as they develop their communication, language and literacy skills. The broad range of activities includes ideas for encouraging children to read and write simple words, create their own books, retell rhymes and stories and investigate letter sounds

GROUP SIZE
Any size.

TIMING
Ten to 15 minutes.

HOME LINKS
Ask the children to bring in one book from home that they have enjoyed to review to the rest of the group. Ask carers if they would be prepared (at a pre-arranged time) to talk to the children about a book that they have read and enjoyed.

MULTICULTURAL LINKS
Provide a selection of multicultural books, such as *Handa's Surprise* by Eileen Browne (Walker Books) or *But Martin!* by June Counsel (Corgi) for the children to look at and review.

I LIKED THIS BOOK

Learning objectives
To use talk to organize feelings, speaking clearly and audibly with confidence and control; to learn about book conventions and show an understanding of the elements of stories.

What you need
A book of your own, either fiction or non-fiction, that you have enjoyed reading; access to a selection of books; cassette recorder; cassette; glue; scrapbook; paper; writing materials.

What to do
Show your book to the children and explain that it is a book that you have read and enjoyed. Tell the children the title and author and then give a brief summary of the book. If the book has any 'blurb' on the back cover you could read this to the children. Explain why you liked the book. For a non-fiction book, maybe the pictures were informative, or the book was about a subject that you are interested in. If you chose a story-book, perhaps the story was exciting and made you wonder what was going to happen next, or the characters seemed like real people.

Ask two or three of the children to find a book that they have enjoyed. Help the children to explain why they liked the book. Were the pictures good – did they tell you more about the story? Was the book funny? Was it a book that they could read by themselves?

Encourage the children to give short reviews of their favourite books. Record the reviews onto a cassette and place them in the book corner with a cassette recorder so that the children can listen to the thoughts of other readers. Alternatively, encourage the children to tell their reviews to an adult who can write them down. Stick the finished reviews into a scrapbook with glue and keep with the reading books.

Support
Use this as a whole-group activity after reading a story to the group. Ask the children if they liked the book. Encourage them to think of as many reasons as possible.

Extension
Ask individuals to choose a book in advance to prepare a review on. Encourage them to give more information about the book such as the author's name and the type of book (fiction or non-fiction).

TONGUE-TWISTERS

Learning objectives
To hear and say initial sounds in words; to link letters and sounds and identify words beginning with the same sound.

What you need
Some tongue-twisters, for example, 'Peter Piper picked a peck of pickled pepper' where almost all the words begin with the same letter or sound; the photocopiable sheet on page 72; large sheet of paper; marker pen; A4 white paper; colouring materials.

What to do
Say a few tongue-twisters to the group. Show the children the photocopiable sheet and read the two tongue-twisters aloud. Choose a short tongue-twister and write it out onto the large sheet of paper, explaining how virtually all of the words begin with the same letter and sound. Repeat the tongue-twisters slowly, pointing to each word as you say it.

Tell the children that you are going to make some more tongue-twisters as a group, using their names. Choose one name, for example, 'Sam'. Ask the children to suggest things that Sam could do that begin with the same letter as his name, such as 'swims' or 'sees' (a verb), and a word that explains how he does that, such as 'slowly' or 'sadly' (an adverb). Give as many children as possible a chance to make up their own tongue-twister. Help the children to write their tongue-twisters down on individual sheets of paper then encourage them to illustrate the pages. Compile these into a book. Encourage the children to become more aware of the initial sounds of objects by making a display of items that all begin with the same sound such as 'bucket', 'ball', 'bear' and 'book'.

Support
Ask the children to think of just one thing that they could do that begins with the same letter or sound as their name. If two or more children have names beginning with the same sound, join the short sentences together to make one long tongue-twister, for example, 'Sam swims, Sue skips and Stephen screams'.

Extension
Challenge the children to try to make long sentences with each word beginning with the same letter. For example, 'Carla crunched carrots carefully'. Remind them that the sentences must make sense!

GROUP SIZE
Pairs or individuals.

TIMING
Five to ten minutes.

HOME LINKS
Ask carers to help their children find two objects that rhyme with each other at home. Let the children draw a picture of the objects and bring it in to show to the rest of the group.

FALL SOUNDS LIKE WALL

Learning objectives

To explore and read familiar and common rhyming words; to compare onsets and rimes and understand how the word changes when the onset changes.

What you need

The photocopiable sheet on page 74; thin card; scissors; glue; copy of the nursery rhyme 'Humpty Dumpty'; plastic covering film (optional); large sheet of paper; marker pen.

Preparation

Copy the photocopiable sheet onto thin card. Cut out each oval shape. If desired, cover the shapes with the plastic film. Cut along the zigzag lines to separate each oval into two pieces.

What to do

Read or recite the rhyme 'Humpty Dumpty' to the children. Explain that 'wall' and 'fall' are rhyming words because they sound the same. Write the words onto a large sheet of paper and show the children that the words look the same too, except they have different initial letters. Can the children think of any more pairs of rhyming words, such as bin and tin or cat and hat? Show the children the half oval with 'wall' written on it. Help them to find the other half, which says 'fall'. Encourage them to look particularly at the end of the word (rime). Remind the children that the end of the word will be the same, but the initial letter changes. When they have found the other half, help them to fit the two pieces together.

Spread the remaining ovals out on a table, separating the halves and mixing them up. Challenge the children to make the ovals whole again. The children will know when they have successfully paired the halves because the ovals will fit together along the zigzag line. Follow up the activity by making a collection of poems and nursery rhymes that contain obvious rhymes, or by having a 'Rhyme of the week', when you choose one word and the children have to try to find as many words as possible that rhyme with that word.

Support

Draw pictures to match the words on the halves of each oval, then let the children use the pictures as clues to the meaning of the words.

Extension

Give the children blank oval shapes. Ask them to draw a zigzag line across the middle of the oval and carefully cut along it with a pair of scissors. Encourage them to think of and write their own pairs of rhyming words onto the two halves of the ovals.

I'LL HUFF AND I'LL PUFF

Learning objectives
To retell narratives in the correct sequence drawing on the language patterns of stories; to develop an understanding of the elements of a story such as the main character and sequence of events.

What you need
Story of 'The Three Little Pigs' (Traditional); props including sticks, straw, plastic bricks and objects to recreate a sitting room and/or dining room such as chairs, table, place settings, magazines and a cardboard box painted to look like a television.

Preparation
Arrange the props in the home corner to look like the three pigs' cottage.

What to do
Read the story of 'The Three Little Pigs' to the group and encourage the children to join in, especially with the refrains 'not by the hair on my chinny chin chin...' and 'I'll huff and I'll puff...'. Talk with the children about the events in the book and the order in which they happened. To help them remember the sequence of events, you could collect a small quantity of each type of building material mentioned in the story and ask the children to try blowing it down!

Show the children the three pigs' cottage that you have created. Initially, the children may need help to re-enact the story. Help them to decide who will be the wolf and who will be each pig. Encourage the children to use the language of the story, including the refrains and repetitions, and the sequence of events to role-play the story, beginning with the house of straw. To help them with their retelling they could make pig and wolf masks, or wear tails made from appropriately-coloured card. When the children are confident, try role-playing other traditional stories such as 'Cinderella', 'Jack and the Beanstalk' or 'Dick Whittington'.

Support
Take on one of the roles from the story yourself until the children are confident with their role-play.

Extension
Ask the children to try to think about how the characters might have felt at each part of the story.

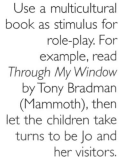

GROUP SIZE
Four to 25 children. (This activity can be carried out with larger numbers, but you will need extra sets of the photocopiable cards.)

TIMING
Five to ten minutes.

HOME LINKS
Ask carers to help their children to write down a list of five to ten things that the household buys each week such as milk, apples, toothpaste or rice, which the children can read to the rest of the group.

I WENT SHOPPING

Learning objectives
To read a range of familiar and common words independently; to link sounds and pictures with letters and words.

What you need
A copy of each of the photocopiable sheets on pages 75, 76 and 77.

Preparation
Cut around each individual picture on the photocopiable sheets to make a set of 26 cards.

What to do
Ask the children to sit in a circle on the floor. Show them the cards one at a time, making sure that they all know what all of the pictures are. Give one card to each child and keep one yourself. Start the game by saying, 'I went shopping and I bought a...' then say the name of the object on your card, for example, 'drum'. Now ask the child sitting next to you to continue by saying, 'I went shopping and I bought a drum and a...' then adding on the name of the object on their card.

Once each child has had their turn they should place their card face up on the floor for the others to refer to. Continue around the circle until everyone has had a turn. Encourage each child to try to read the word underneath their picture too.

To make the game more realistic, ask each child to bring in an itemized shopping receipt showing food or general household items. Look together at the types of items bought and make your own cards based on the objects, with illustrations by the children.

Support
Ask each child to add only the item on the card of the previous child to their shopping list.

Extension
Encourage the children to read the words only by covering up the pictures on the cards. Gradually give the children fewer clues about the meaning of the word.

GROUP SIZE
Any size.

TIMING
Five to ten minutes.

HOME LINKS
Ask carers to help
their children find
and read initials and
acronyms around
the home such as
BBC or BT.

KC MEETS JD

Learning objectives

To develop awareness of initial sounds in words and hear and say them; to link sounds to letters.

What you need

Just the children!

What to do

Sit the children in a circle. Explain to the group that an initial is the first letter of a word. It may help to give the children some examples, such as London has an initial of 'L' and apple has an initial of 'a'. Tell the group that sometimes, especially on mail, people's names are shortened to just their initials. For example, Laura Bell might be called Miss L Bell. Occasionally, on labels for example, other names can be reduced to initials too, such as KC or JD.

Explain to the children that everyone is going to have a chance to say what their initials are. Start the activity yourself by saying, 'I am...' and include your title, initial and family name. Let the children continue around the circle, taking it in turns to say their own initials.

MULTICULTURAL LINKS
Make simple cards
showing names
from other cultures
(not those of
children in the
group) such as
Chatchai
Pongsawong or
Randjit Singh. Show
the cards one at a
time to the group
and ask them to
decide what the
initials are for each
of the names.

Look further at initials by showing the group examples of signatures on prints of paintings. Let the children experiment with their initials and signatures by making 'cheque books' from strips of paper. Use the cheque books in role-play shops, travel agents and theatres to pay for food, tickets and so on.

Support

Ask the children to say just the initial for their first name and to give their full family name, for example B Cann, without giving the prefix 'I am...'.

Some of the children may need extra help to know what letter their name begins with (small cards with each child's name on can help here), and to match the phonic sound of their name with the alphabet sound of the capital.

Extension

Encourage each child to say, 'I am... and next to me is...', adding the initials of the people on either side of them.

I WROTE THAT BOOK

Learning objectives
To write and read a range of familiar words; to learn about the processes involved in making a book.

What you need
Sheets of A4 white paper; drawing materials; picture book such as *Dr Xargle's Book of Earthlets* by Jeanne Willis and Tony Ross (Red Fox).

What to do
Show the children the picture book and explain to them who the author and illustrator are. Look through the book together to see where the pictures and words are on each page. Arrange the children into pairs (if necessary, this activity could be done with larger group sizes) and explain that each pair is going to make a book. In their pairs, ask the children to decide who will write the story and who will draw the illustrations. Provide plenty of paper and writing and drawing materials, then let them work on their story for as long as necessary. This may take two or three sessions, especially if the children choose to write several drafts of the book.

When the children have finished their stories, help them to make the individual pages into a book. The pages could be stapled together, stuck into a scrapbook, or tied with a piece of ribbon. Ask the author and illustrator to read their book to the rest of the group.

As an alternative to writing a story, the children could write books about topics such as 'Cars', 'Our house', or 'My favourite toy', or they could try rewriting picture books that they enjoy such as *The Very Hungry Caterpillar* by Eric Carle (Hamish Hamilton). Help to develop the children's awareness of authors and illustrators by making collections of the work of certain authors and illustrators such as Quentin Blake, Mick Inkpen or Shirley Hughes.

The mouse who liked to eat lots of cheese

Support
Help the children to write down their story, possibly acting as a scribe so that they are able to see the link between the spoken and written word.

Extension
Encourage the children to work individually to make their own books, being both author and illustrator.

Ask the children to think carefully about what their story is going to be about before they begin writing and to decide on the sequence of events.

GROUP SIZE
Any size.

TIMING
Five to ten minutes.

FIND THE WORD CARDS

Learning objectives

To read a range of familiar words; to link letters and sounds.

What you need

Small cards (blank playing cards are ideal); marker pen.

Preparation

Write one short word, such as 'dog' or 'cat' on each card. (Allow three to four cards per child and keep a list of the words for your reference.) 'Hide' the cards around the room on shelves, chairs and so on, placing them in accessible places where they can be easily found.

What to do

Explain to the children that you have hidden some cards with words on around the room and you would like the children to try to find them. Give them a time limit, such as five minutes, to find the words. Encourage the children to walk sensibly around the room and tell them that they must not snatch the cards from each other. Try to ensure that everyone finds at least one card. You may also want to give clues as to the position of the cards.

When the children have collected all the cards, ask them to sit down. Using your list, read out the words one at a time. Ask the children to tell you if they have a card with the word that you have just read out. Encourage them to look at the initial, shape and length of each word and to look for spelling patterns.

As an alternative, ask the whole group to help you to write a short story with two or three sentences. Copy each word onto a separate piece of card and hide them around the room. Ask the children, in small groups, to find the words and recreate the story.

Make this a regular activity by choosing one word each week, and asking the children to find as many examples of that word as possible around the room, in books, in magazines, on signs and so on.

Support

Call the children out one at a time to read to you the words that they have found. Encourage them to sound out the letters and any vowel or consonant combinations.

Extension

Ask each child to choose one of the cards that they have found, and to make a sentence containing that word.

HOME LINKS
For each child, write two or three words onto a piece of paper that they find difficult to read. Next to each word write a sentence containing that word, for example, 'like' and 'I like ice-cream.' Ask carers to help their children to read the words and the sentences.

GROUP SIZE
Four to six children.

TIMING
Ten to 15 minutes.

HOME LINKS
When writing cards, ask carers to involve their children as much as possible, showing the children their names and reading the verses and messages together.

MULTICULTURAL LINKS
Look at cards for multicultural celebrations such as Divali and Hanukkah. A variety of cards for different occasions can be obtained from Religion in Evidence, TTS, Monk Road, Alfreton, Derbyshire DE55 7RL. Tel: 0800-318686.

I AM FIVE

Learning objectives
To write their own names and form sentences; to read familiar words, symbols and own name.

What you need
Selection of greetings cards; A4 card in a variety of colours; drawing and writing materials; decorating materials including glitter glue, gummed paper shapes, fabric or other materials (optional).

Preparation
Two or three days in advance, ask carers if they could provide old greetings cards for the children to look at together.

What to do
Sit with a group of children and look together at the cards that they have brought from home. Talk about the types of cards and the different events that they are for. Help the group to sort the cards into type – put all the Christmas cards together, all the birthday cards and so on. Encourage the children to look at the pictures and try to read the words as they sort the cards. Read any rhymes and messages inside the cards.

Ask each child in turn to think of a card that they would like to make – it could be a Mother's Day card, a thank-you card or a friendship card. Let them choose a piece of card and help them to fold it into the desired shape. Ask the children to draw an appropriate picture and to think of the writing that they wish to add to the card for the event that they have chosen. If necessary, help the children to find the words that they need on the commercial cards. If the children are decorating their cards, provide a selection of materials for them to choose from such as glitter, gummed paper and fabric scraps.

Once the cards are finished, display them and ask the children to read them and decide what each card is celebrating.

Support
Choose four or five cards in advance that have short, simple verses inside. Make two or three copies of the verses then give these to the children and read them together as a group. You may need to act as a scribe once the children have composed their writing.

Extension
Ask each child in the group to read a verse by themselves. Encourage the children to write more independently on their cards.

HOME LINKS
Encourage carers to
tell nursery rhymes
to their children,
such as 'Incy Wincy
Spider' or 'I Had a
Little Nut Tree', and
to ask the children
to join in as much
as possible while
listening for the
rhymes in each
poem.

**MULTICULTURAL
LINKS**
Look at
multicultural rhyme
books such as *Give
Yourself a Hug* by
Grace Nichols
(Puffin).

OUR RHYME BOOK

Learning objectives
To retell rhymes using appropriate language and sequencing, speaking audibly and with confidence and control; to link sounds with patterns in rhymes and to read familiar words.

What you need
Paper (in your choice of colour, size and shape depending on how you want the final book to look); writing and drawing materials.

Preparation
Have ready four or five nursery rhymes such as 'Dr Foster', 'Little Miss Muffet' or 'Polly Put the Kettle On' which you could read or recite to the group, or a rhyme book such as *Oranges and Lemons* by Karen King and Ian Beck (Oxford University Press).

What to do
Read or recite the rhymes to the group. Ask the children if they know of any rhymes that they could tell to the rest of the group. Choose a rhyme that most of the children are familiar with that contains a name, such as 'Polly Put the Kettle On', and ask them to say the rhyme, substituting their own name for the name of the nursery rhyme character. Once each child has tried this, ask them to think of a name that sounds like the one in the rhyme (it could be a nonsense name). Try this with a variety of rhymes containing names.

Work with small groups of four to six children to write the new rhymes down. Encourage the children to copy-write or write independently. Invite the children to illustrate their work. Compile all the rhymes together and make them into a book, perhaps by sticking them into a scrapbook or by stapling the pages together. Add the title 'Our rhyme book'.

Support
Rather than writing all the rhymes down on paper, ask the children to say them into a microphone and record them onto an audio cassette.

Extension
Ask the children to replace other words in the rhymes. For example, replace the word 'spider' in 'Little Miss Muffet' with the word 'camel'. Ideally, encourage the children to keep the rhythm of the rhyme, and, if possible, to think of words that rhyme, too.

CHAPTER 3

Mathematical development

Develop the children's mathematical understanding using the range of practical activities in this chapter. Ideas include using stories to investigate pattern and sequence, role-play games to develop mathematical vocabulary and recipe ideas to encourage comparative language

GROUP SIZE
Four to six children.

TIMING
Five to ten minutes.

HOME LINKS
Ask the children to draw a picture of a favourite toy at home and to write a sentence explaining where the toy is kept.

IT'S IN THE BOX

Learning objectives
To use everyday words to describe position; to read common words, matching written and spoken words, and develop an understanding of sentence construction.

What you need
A teddy bear or other animal soft toy; a number of objects that the toy could fit on, under, behind and so on, such as a chair, box or book; several sheets of A4 white card; marker pen; scissors.

Preparation
Cut the white card into strips and cut some strips in half to make smaller cards. On the long strips, write out sentences such as 'Teddy is _____ the box', mentioning the object and name of the toy, and leaving a blank space for the preposition (on, in, under and so on). In the same size writing, write one positional word on each of the smaller pieces of card.

What to do
Show the toy to the children and place it in the box. Show them the sentences and words. Help the children to find the sentence with the name of the object in it, for example, 'Teddy is _____ the box' and to find the correct positional word to fill the blank. Let the children take turns to place the toy close to an object that you have chosen, and to find the correct sentence and preposition to match the toy's location.

Alternatively, hide the teddy in the room. Let the children try to find it by giving them clues to the teddy's position. This can also be adapted for a simple warm-up activity by calling out instructions for the children, such as 'stand next to someone with blue eyes' or 'sit on your hands'.

Support
Provide just the positional words on cards. Ask individual children to place the toy near an object and to find a word to describe where the toy is.

Extension
Give the children a pre-determined selection of objects. Write out the sentences as for the main activity, but cut up the sentences so that each word is on a separate piece of card. Let the children decide where to put the toy. Ask the children to find the words to make a sentence explaining the toy's position.

TUESDAY IS COOKING DAY

Learning objectives
To read numerals 1 to 9 and times and sequence events and days of the week; to read familiar and common words and simple sentences independently.

What you need
Seven large sheets of paper (at least A3 size); marker pens or felt-tipped pens in a variety of colours; a variety of objects with times and dates such as old diaries, calendars, bus timetables and television guides.

What to do
Explain to the children that you want to make a diary for the wall to help everyone remember what happens each day during your sessions. Look at the diaries, calendars, timetables and television guides with the children and discuss the sequence of days and months.

Take one of the large sheets of paper and write 'Monday' at the top of it with a marker pen. Divide the sheet into sections depending on the breaks in the session and what you want to include, for example, registration, activity time, snack time and story-time. With the children's help, write the events for Monday under the heading, and the times that they happen. Repeat for the other days, starting each one on a new sheet of paper. For Saturday and Sunday, ask the children what they do at the weekend and then write down their suggestions, for example, 'Billy goes swimming' or Hassan rides his bike'. Ask the children to provide illustrations. Each day, choose a child to change the page in the diary and read what is written there.

Support
Write one activity down for each day, such as 'Tuesday is cooking day'. Let the children draw pictures to accompany each sentence.

Extension
Let the children make their own diaries from two sheets of A4 paper folded in half, with one piece of paper inserted inside the other. Use one page for each day.

GROUP SIZE
Any size.

TIMING
Ten minutes (or longer if desired).

FOUR ORANGES, PLEASE!

Learning objectives

To begin to use the vocabulary involved in adding and subtracting and have the opportunity to use money; to learn about the alphabet and read familiar words.

What you need

Sheets of white A4 card; scissors; drawing and writing materials; equipment to set up a greengrocer's in the role-play area including a selection of pretend fruit (either plastic or made by the children from clay and then painted); table; weighing scales; till; play money; shopping baskets; white A4 paper.

Preparation

Make price cards by cutting a sheet of A4 card into smaller sections. Set up a greengrocer's in the role-play area using the table as a counter. Find an area for the 'wholesaler' in the room. Make some blank order forms with spaces for the children to write on what they need to buy from the wholesaler, and the quantity required.

What to do

Show the role-play area to the group and explain that it is a greengrocer's. Show the children the play fruit and vegetables and ask them to decide what they would like to sell in the shop. Leave the rest of the items at the 'wholesalers'. Help the group to make an alphabetical catalogue listing all of the items in the shop by writing the names of the fruit and vegetables on individual sheets of card. Ask the children to draw pictures of the produce next to the appropriate items. Count the quantity of each item and write the numbers on the appropriate cards next to the pictures. Help the children to decide how much each item should cost, then make labels showing the name of each fruit or vegetable and its price. Explain that, when the shop is closed, the 'greengrocer' has to visit the 'wholesaler' to buy more produce, taking an order form.

Once the shop is fully stocked, it can open to customers. Starting with a fully-stocked shop, ask one child to be the greengrocer, one to be the wholesaler and six children to be customers. Encourage the customers to visit the shop with pretend money and buy various items of food. Encourage the greengrocer to count the money and provide change if necessary. When the greengrocer has sold most of the stock, he should visit the wholesaler with an order form to restock the shop. Let different children take the role of the greengrocer, deciding when to shut the shop and restock it.

HOME LINKS
Tell carers about the role-play area and ask them to include their children when they visit a greengrocer's, pointing out the different items and prices.

MULTICULTURAL LINKS
Include exotic fruits and vegetables like mango and okra in the catalogue. Show the real items to the children and try eating them too.

Support

Keep each type of fruit and vegetable to a maximum of ten and have fewer entries in the catalogue. Make the prices low initially, using just '1p' and '2p' price tags.

Extension

Increase the prices and have more entries in the catalogue.

GROUP SIZE
Six children, and one 'caller'.

TIMING
Ten to 15 minutes.

TRIANGLE BEGINS WITH 'T'

Learning objectives

To read shape names and use language to describe flat shapes; to read familiar words, looking at the shape and length of the word.

What you need

Up to 12 copies of the photocopiable sheet on page 78, copied onto thin card (two per player); variety of 2-D and 3-D shapes; laminating materials (optional).

Preparation

Cut six of the photocopiable sheets into individual squares to make the playing pieces. If desired, laminate the uncut copies and small squares. Use the 2-D and 3-D shapes to make a display in the room. Label each shape with its name and a sentence explaining its properties, for example, 'A triangle has 3 corners'.

What to do

Show the children the shape display and talk about the different shapes and their properties. You may want to ask the children to find further examples of each shape to add to the display. Nominate a caller and give each of the players a baseboard. Turn the cut-out pieces face down and place them in a pile in front of the caller. Explain to the players that they have to match the words on their board with the cards that the caller shows them. The caller should turn the first card over and show it to the rest of the group. The first player to correctly identify the shape by saying its name

keeps the piece and places it on top of the correct shape on their board.

Encourage the children to look closely at the shape of the initial letter and the overall shape of the word. Are there any tall letters? Are there any letters that have tails? Is it a long or short word? The winner is the first person to cover all the shapes on their baseboard.

Support

Ask the caller to show each child in turn one of the small cards. Encourage the children to look at the picture for help with the meaning of the word.

Extension

Cover the pictures with a piece of gummed paper so that the children have to look closely at the shapes of the word themselves.

HOME LINKS
Give each child a copy of the words from the game to take home. Ask carers to help their children to try to find an example of each shape at home, and to label it with the correct word.

GROUP SIZE
Up to six children.

TIMING
Five to ten minutes.

HOME LINKS
Ask carers to help their children to find two or three rhyming words that could be shared with the rest of the group, or encourage them to look safely at car number plates with their children when they are walking around their local area.

NUMBER PLATE WORDS

Learning objectives
To talk about, read and recreate simple sound patterns; to hear and say initial and final sounds in words and short vowel sounds within words.

What you need
A copy of the photocopiable sheet on page 79, copied onto thin card; scissors; sheet of A4 paper; pen.

Preparation
Cut out the individual number plates from the photocopiable sheet.

What to do
On a sheet of A4 paper, make up a simple number plate for example, 'B456 OOT'. Tell the children that, sometimes, the letters in a number plate make a word. Cover the numbers in the number plate and show the children the word 'BOOT'. Explain that with some words, the first letter (onset or initial) can be changed with another letter to make a new word, for example swap the 'b' for an 'f' to make the word 'foot'. Remind the children that the sound at the end of the word (rime) remains the same even though the first letter changes.

Show the children the number plate cards from the photocopiable sheet and give one card to each child. Make sure that everyone knows the word that is 'hidden' on their number plate. Let the children have a couple of minutes to try to think of some words that sound the same as the word on their plate, but have a different beginning sound. Once the group has had chance to think of some words, ask the children to share the words that they have found. When the children have had some practice at this, encourage them to make up their own number plates containing words.

Support
Ask the children to say aloud just the words that they find. Encourage them to experiment with sounds and to combine the end of each word with the phonic sounds they know. Some of the words may be nonsensical.

Extension
Ask the children to write down all the words that they can think of that sound like the word on their number plate. Encourage them to use a dictionary to check the meaning of any words that they are uncertain about.

GROUP SIZE
Four to six children.

TIMING
Ten to 20 minutes.

HOME LINKS
Ask carers to help their children to make simple addition and subtraction sums using everyday objects such as utensils, books, fruit and so on.

MULTICULTURAL LINKS
Make up some number stories yourself that use names (such as Kezia or Maya) or objects (such as sari or turban) from other cultures. Display the stories around the room.

NUMBER STORIES

Learning objectives

To begin to relate addition to combining two groups of objects and subtraction to taking away; to develop an understanding of sequencing and directionality of print and read familiar words.

What you need

Flip chart or large sheet of paper on an easel; marker pens; A4 sheets of paper; drawing and writing materials.

Preparation

If desired, you could write or draw a number story in advance.

What to do

Sit the children so that they can all see the large sheet of paper or flip chart. Explain that you are going to make up a story and draw pictures to illustrate each part (sentence) of it. (Essentially, the story will be a simple sum.) The pictures can be as simple or as detailed as you like. For example, 'Joe has 3 books' – draw a picture of Joe holding three books next to the sentence; 'Fatima has 4 books' – draw a picture of Fatima holding four books next to that sentence; 'Together they have 7 books' – draw a picture of Joe and Fatima with the seven books in between them. Ask two or three of the children to suggest simple stories, using adding or taking away, which could be drawn. Give each child an A4 sheet of paper. Encourage them to draw their 'stories' and help them to write the appropriate sentences. Let the children read each other's stories.

Once the children are familiar with writing number stories, let them cut out pictures of people and objects from old catalogues. Provide a selection of names, numbers and simple words on individual pieces of card that the children can use to make sentences. Ask them to mix and match the pictures to make number stories.

Support

Rather than writing the stories down, let the children just draw the pictures – perhaps showing someone giving something to another person – and then encourage them to 'read' their story to a friend.

Extension

Encourage the children to write longer stories, perhaps using more characters and using larger numbers for the adding and subtracting.

GROUP SIZE
Four to six children.

TIMING
Ten to 20 minutes.

THINK OF A RECIPE

Learning objectives
To read and write numerals 1 to 9, and use comparative language such as 'more', 'less', 'heavier' and 'lighter'; to read familiar and common words and simple sentences independently.

What you need
Some recipe books in an easy-to-read format with pictures; *Roald Dahl's Revolting Recipes* by Roald Dahl (Red Fox); sheets of A3 paper; drawing and writing materials.

Preparation
Look through the recipe books for one very simple recipe such as Welsh rabbit or a flavoured milkshake.

What to do
Show the group the recipe that you have chosen and look at the instructions for making the food. Discuss the format for a recipe: a list of ingredients, details of equipment needed, and a method that tells you what to do. Explain to the children that you would like them to help you make up a recipe.

Show the children *Roald Dahl's Revolting Recipes* and talk about the fantastical ingredients. As a group, discuss the type of recipe that the children would like to write. Would it be for a cake, a drink or maybe a pizza? Help them to decide on a name for their creation and write it on a sheet of A3 paper. Underneath the recipe name, write a list of ingredients and a method for making the dish. Encourage the children to think about the quantities of ingredients needed. Do they need more or less of one item than another? Help the group to sequence the method of the recipe. Ask the children to take it in turns to add suitable illustrations to the recipe sheet.

Once all of the children in your group have had a chance to contribute to a recipe, put copies of the recipes, cooking utensils (wooden spoons, pans and so on) and pretend food in the role-play area for the children to try reading and making the recipes.

HOME LINKS
Ask carers to include their children in cooking activities, helping them to read the recipe, weigh ingredients and stir the mixture.

MULTICULTURAL LINKS
Look together at books about multicultural food such as *Breakfast Around the World* by Gill Munton (Wayland).

Support
Help the children to make up a recipe verbally. Give each child a sheet of A5 paper and ask them to draw a different part of the recipe, such as the ingredients needed, or the mixing stage. Glue the sheets in sequence on a large piece of card.

Extension
Ask the children to write their own recipes independently, using dictionaries to check spellings.

SORT THE WRAPPERS

Learning objectives

To use language such as 'more', 'less', 'greater' or 'heavier' and sort objects by weight; to read familiar words and numbers.

What you need

Clean wrappers from a selection of foodstuffs such as chocolate wrappers, crisp packets, empty yoghurt pots, cereal boxes (ideally, there should be a variety of weights for each food type); price labels marked '1p', '5p' and '10p'; variety of sizes of boxes; sheets of plain paper; felt-tipped pens; number squares listing numbers from 1 to 100 in chronological order.

Preparation

Two or three days in advance, ask carers if they could provide clean packaging and wrappers, but not plastic bags.

What to do

With the children's help, sort the packaging into piles by type – all the crisps together, all the chocolate together and so on. Choose one crisp packet and show the children the weight printed on it. Tell the children what the 'g' stands for.

Explain to the group that you would like to know which packet of crisps has the greatest weight on it, and which has the smallest. As a group, help the children to find the weights on each of the packets, and to decide which are the heaviest and lightest packs. Use the number squares to show the children which are the largest and smallest numbers. Now show the children the price labels. Explain that you are going to give the biggest packs of crisps the highest price (10p), the smallest packs the lowest price (1p) and the remaining packets the 5p price tags. Put the expensive crisps in one box, the cheapest crisps in another box and so on. Ask the children to write appropriate labels for each box. Sort the remaining wrappers in the same way.

Use the boxes and wrappers to create a 'snack bar' in the role-play area for the children to buy and sell food. Include pretend fruit and healthy snacks for the children to buy.

Support

Give the children just two different price labels – '1p' and '5p'. You could also make the '1p' tags much smaller in size than the '5p' labels. Provide wrappers with small weights, ideally less than 20/30g or ml.

Extension

Give the children higher priced labels and larger weights, with numbers up to 100 or even higher.

BILLY GOATS GRUFF

Learning objectives
To say and use number names in familiar contexts; to show an understanding of pattern and sequence of events in stories.

What you need
A copy of the photocopiable sheet on page 69.

Preparation
Read the story through so that you are familiar with it.

What to do
Read the story 'Billy Goats Gruff' on the photocopiable sheet to the children. Talk about the repetition in the story each time that one of the goats wants to cross the bridge. Re-read the story and ask the children to join in with the repetitions. Choose one child to be the troll and three to be the goats. Ask the children to line up, and then introduce themselves by saying, 'I'm the first, and smallest, Billy Goat Gruff...'; 'I'm the second Billy Goat Gruff' and so on. Re-read the story, encouraging the children playing the troll and the goats to join in at the appropriate time. For even more audience participation, increase the number of goats crossing the bridge to, perhaps, seven Billy Goats Gruff!

When the children have had a chance to practise the sequence of the story a few times, let them make masks from paper plates for the goats and troll to wear, and use different voices for each goat. The smallest goat might have a quiet squeaky voice, and the third billy goat might have a loud, booming voice.

Support
To help the children remember which goat they are, and reinforce recognition of written numbers, give each goat a card with their number written on it to hold while they tell the story.

Extension
Write each ordinal number from first to tenth on an individual piece of card. Decide with the children the number of goats needed to retell the story and choose that number of children. Allocate a number to each child and then ask them to find the card with their number written on it. Once everyone has their card, ask the children to organize themselves into a line in the correct order.

GROUP SIZE
Two to four children.

TIMING
Five to ten minutes.

HOME LINKS
Ask carers to encourage their children to count at home, such as counting the number of shirts hanging on the washing line or the apples in the fruit bowl.

MULTICULTURAL LINKS
Find out whether any carers or helpers can count to ten in another language and ask them to teach this to the children.

TEN, NINE, EIGHT...

Learning objectives
To count using up to ten objects; to read names and familiar words.

What you need
Ten in the Bed by Penny Dale (Walker Books); large, shallow cardboard box; doll's pillow and sheet or duvet; variety of soft toys brought from home by the children; a few spare toys.

Preparation
Two or three days in advance, ask carers if each child could each bring a soft toy from home. Ask them to write a label giving the name of the child and the type of toy, such as 'Sophie's rabbit' or 'Sinead's cat', and to tape it securely to the front of the toy so the writing can be easily seen.

What to do
Read *Ten in the Bed* to the children. Look together at the illustrations and count the animals in the bed on each page. Show the children the cardboard box with the doll's pillow and duvet, and explain that it is a 'bed' for some of the soft toys. As a group, say the rhyme again. Ask one child to put the appropriate number of animals in the bed and say what each toy is and who it belongs to, for example, 'There are six in the bed: Jack's elephant, Eve's teddy...'. When you reach the part in the rhyme where one toy falls out of bed, let the child remove one of the animals from the box, then count together the number of toys left. Take all the toys from the box and let another child put the next number of toys in the bed and continue naming them and taking one out.

Support
Rather than having ten in the bed, work with a smaller number such as five or three.

Extension
Make the rhyme longer, maybe twenty in the bed. Let the children take turns to put the toys in the bed. To keep the activity short, rather than reading the labels on all the toys, ask the children to read some of them, perhaps alternate labels, or the label on every third toy put in the box.

CHAPTER 4

Knowledge and understanding of the world

In this chapter you will find ideas for a range of activities that make use of the resources in the children's immediate surroundings and in the wider world. Activities include looking at weather symbols, taking an observation walk to find different types of print and talking about past events in the children's lives

GROUP SIZE
Any size.

TIMING
Fifteen to 20 minutes for walk, five to ten minutes for activity at setting.

HOME LINKS
Ask carers to write down their children's addresses and telephone numbers and to help them to try to read and remember them.

READ THE SIGNS

Learning objectives
To observe and identify features in the place that they live; to link letters and sounds, understanding that both pictures and words carry meaning.

What you need
Paper; pencils; clipboards; card; writing and colouring materials; chalk; camera and film (optional); masking tape; safe, open area (either indoors or outside); play vehicles (optional).

Preparation
Several days before carrying out this activity, ask carers if they would like to accompany the children on an observation walk. Walk around the local area yourself, noting different types of print and the locations at which you found them, for example shop and house names, advertising hoardings or writing on the side of vehicles. Plan your route so that the children can see as much writing and print as possible.

What to do
Tell the children that you are all going on a walk to look for writing, numbers and letters, and that you would like them to draw a picture of a sign that they see and like. Give the children clipboards, paper and pencils.

During the walk, draw the children's attention to the letters and signs around them and talk about why some signs, such as road signs, are important. Encourage them to look for examples of signs and writing everywhere, even under their feet. Ask them to choose one sign and to carefully copy the shapes, colour and writing. Back at your setting, help the children, in groups of four to six, to copy their designs onto card.

Draw some chalk roads on an outside area or use a large clear space indoors. Tape some of the children's signs around the area. If possible, provide play vehicles such as bikes or lorries, then encourage the children to travel around the 'local area' visiting some of the places that they saw during their walk and read the signs that they pass.

Support
Encourage the children to focus on the colours and pictures on the signs rather than the writing.

Extension
Ask the children to focus particularly on the writing on the signs.

IT'S SUNNY

Learning objectives

To observe and identify features in the natural world; to read a range of familiar words and develop a sight vocabulary for words about the weather.

What you need

Weather forecasts from newspapers (showing maps of the country if possible); the photocopiable sheet on page 80; large map of your regional area (A3 or larger if possible); Blu-Tack; laminating materials (optional).

Preparation

Copy the photocopiable sheet four times onto card. If desired, laminate the sheets, then cut out the sections to make individual word and picture cards. Mount the large map at child height.

What to do

Explain to the children that, sometimes, people like to know what the weather will be for the following day or week so that they can plan the clothes that they might wear, visits that they might make and jobs that they could do, such as washing the car or cleaning the windows. Ask the group if they, or their carers, watch weather forecasts on television or read them in a paper. Talk with the children about what they know about weather forecasts. If the children have no ideas, show them the forecasts cut from the papers and read them to the group. Discuss the meaning of any words that the children are unsure about.

Now show the children the map, and using the symbol cards, make a mock weather forecast by sticking the symbols onto the map with Blu-Tack in the relevant places. Let the children take turns to try to be the weather forecaster, using a variety of symbols and weather conditions in their forecasts.

Support

Give the children the weather symbols rather than the words. Ask them to draw alternative pictures for each weather condition, such as a snowman for snow or an umbrella for rain.

Extension

Using the words from the photocopiable sheet, let the children write down their forecasts, then read them to the rest of the group. Look on the map for names of towns where the children's friends and relatives live, then encourage them to use these in their weather forecasts.

GROUP SIZE
Four to six children.

TIMING
Ten to 30 minutes.

HOME LINKS
Ask carers to talk with their children about pets and animals they see, and to help the children think of words to describe the animals.

ANIMAL PASSPORTS

Learning objectives
To identify some of the features of living things; to learn about how a book is organized and read familiar words.

What you need
White A4 paper; drawing and writing materials; variety of books about animals that include simple text and large pictures (photographs if possible), such as *The Big Book of Animals* (Dorling Kindersley).

Preparation
Fold each sheet of A4 paper into quarters – you will need one per child. Make a prototype 'passport' from one of the folded sheets. On the front, write 'passport' and draw a picture of the animal that the passport is about, such as a tiger or an elephant. Inside the passport, include details of what the animal looks like (hair colour, eye colour, size and so on).

What to do
Ask the group if anyone has ever been abroad. Does anyone have a passport? Explain that we use a passport to tell people who we are when we are travelling, to identify us and to keep a record of where we have travelled. Tell the children that they are each going to make a 'passport', but that rather than make one for themselves, they are each going to make one for an animal. Show the group your completed passport.

Ask each child which animal they would like to write about. Give everyone a folded sheet of paper and some drawing and writing materials. Help the children to look through the books to find out more about their chosen animal. Once the children have enough information, encourage them to use your example for guidance as they write about their animal and draw a picture of it on their 'passport'. Display all the finished 'passports' and encourage the children to look at them to find out more about different animals and to discover similarities and differences between them. The details about the animals could then be used as a stimulus for descriptive poems about animals, or to discuss pet care.

Support
Keep the passports very simple. You may want to make a photocopiable passport which already has 'hair colour...', 'eye colour...' and so on written on it for the children to complete.

Extension
Encourage the children to include more details, such as where the animals live and what they like to eat.

GROUP SIZE
Four to six children.

TIMING
Ten to 20 minutes.

HEADLINE NEWS

Learning objectives

To talk about past events in own life; to develop knowledge of directionality of print, sentence conventions and the one-to-one correspondence of written and spoken words linking letters and sounds.

What you need

Two or three newspapers with a variety of headlines; A4 white paper; pencils or black felt-tipped pens.

Preparation

Cut out some of the headlines from the newspapers, ideally ones that the children will be able to read.

What to do

Show the group the headlines that you have cut from the papers and help the children to read them. Explain that headlines have to get the reader's attention – so they are usually in big letters, and use as few words as possible. Ask the children, one at a time, to tell you one thing that they enjoyed doing at the weekend. For example, someone may say, 'I went swimming', or somebody may have had a birthday. Once everyone has thought of something that they did, help the children to make up a 'headline' to tell others about the event. 'I went swimming' could become 'Oliver goes swimming at local leisure centre', or 'Oliver swims across the pool for the first time!'. The headlines could include details about where the children went, who they met, or whether anything interesting happened during the event. Remind the children that headlines usually use names, not 'I'.

Ask the children to write their headlines onto white paper using black pencils or felt-tipped pens. Display these on a board, and encourage the children to read each other's headlines. Have a weekly rota where three or four children write a headline about what they did at the weekend and then read this out to the rest of the group.

Support

Ask the children to phrase a headline and then write this down for them.

Extension

Ask the children to write a short 'article' consisting of perhaps two or three sentences, that tells the reader more about the headline. Add a date, and black and white pictures drawn by the children to turn the headlines into a newspaper.

HOME LINKS
Ask carers to look at newspapers and magazines with their children and to read headlines together.

MULTICULTURAL LINKS
Make a display of newspapers in other languages such as *Die Zeit* and *Le Monde* (available from many local newsagents).

GROUP SIZE
Individuals, or groups of two or three children.

TIMING
Five to ten minutes.

CALCULATED WORDS

Learning objectives
To use everyday technology to support their learning; to compare and read different styles of letters, linking letters and sounds.

What you need
One calculator per child; pencils; paper; collection of objects (or pictures of items) that have digital numbers and letters such as alarm clocks, watches and videos.

What to do
Show the children the pictures and objects that have digital numbers and letters. Discuss the shape of the numbers and letters. Give each child a calculator. Ask them to turn it on (if necessary) and to press some of the number keys. Once the children have done this, ask them to turn the calculator around so that they are now looking at the numbers on the display upside-down. Ask the children if they can read any words on the display! Explain that some numbers, when written digitally and viewed upside-down, can look like letters. For example, '0' looks similar to an 'O', '1' could be an 'I', '2' is a stylized 'Z', '3' could be pressed for 'E', '4' looks similar to an 'h', '5' is an 'S', '6' could be a 'g', '7' an 'L' and '8' a 'B'. Let the children try pressing the relevant buttons, turning the calculator around, looking at the letters and telling each other what they have found.

Now ask the children to experiment and find out how many words they can make using the 'letters' on the calculator. Some words to try include 'egg' (663), 'shell' (77345), 'hole' (3704) and 'log' (607). Encourage the children to write down the words that they find and to compare them with those found by the others in the group.

Support
Help the children to write down the numbers that they see on the upside-down calculator display so that they look more like everyday letters, and are more readable.

Extension
Ask the children to write down the numbers that they input, rather than the words. Ask them to challenge their friends to decide what word the number will become once the calculator is turned upside-down.

HOME LINKS
Ask carers to help their children look for digital displays around the home on videos, microwaves and so on and to read the numbers.

MULTICULTURAL LINKS
Investigate number symbols and words from other languages and use these to make a display.

GROUP SIZE
Four to six children.

TIMING
Ten to 30 minutes (longer if desired).

A BOOK ABOUT PLANTS

Learning objectives
To observe and talk about the features of living things; to learn about book conventions, and read and write familiar words and sentences.

What you need
Some examples of books about plants; two or three plants that the children can look at (potted plants, or some in the local area); pale green paper; drawing and writing materials; scissors; brightly-coloured paper; tape.

Preparation
Make a prototype book following the diagram.

What to do
Share the plant books with the children and talk about their content. Show the children the potted plants or those in the local area. Talk about and identify the different parts of a plant such as stem, petals and leaves, then talk about how plants grow. Explain to the children that they are going to write a book about plants, and show them your example book. Ask each child in turn what they would like to put in their book – it could describe plants that they like, an observation of one of the plants, or a comparison between two of the plants.

Give the children three or four sheets of green paper to make the bulk of their book, and tell them that they should write or draw on one side of the paper only. Provide help as necessary, scribing the children's sentences for them, otherwise let them work as independently as possible, using the information books for reference.

Help each child to draw around the flower template onto a sheet of brightly-coloured paper and use this to make the first page of the book, then tape the rest of the pages together. Fold the pages concertina-style to make a zigzag book. Encourage the children to share their completed books with each other.

This activity could be easily extended by planting some mustard and cress, or broad beans, and using individual pages of a long zigzag book to note the changes as the plant grows.

Support
Act as a scribe for the children. Keep the book short, perhaps with just one piece of stem and a flower head.

Extension
Encourage the children to write more, and to use correct plant terms such as root, stem and so on.

HOME LINKS
Ask carers to look at the trees and plants in the local area with their children. Encourage them to name the plants, talk about their parts and discuss the changes that happen to them each season.

MULTICULTURAL LINKS
Find pictures of plants that are grown and/or eaten in other countries such as tea and bananas.

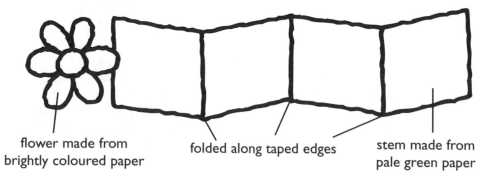

flower made from brightly coloured paper

folded along taped edges

stem made from pale green paper

GROUP SIZE
Any size.

TIMING
Ten to 15 minutes.

WHEN I WAS YOUNGER

Learning objectives
To talk about their families and past events in their own lives; to read familiar words and sentences.

What you need
Pictures of the children when they were younger; examples of photograph albums and baby books; sheets of A4 paper; black felt-tipped pens; large sheets of paper; scrapbook; glue.

Preparation
A few days in advance, ask carers if they could let you have copies of photographs of their children when they were younger. Ask them to tell their children what was happening in their picture and how old they were when it was taken.

What to do
Show the children the photograph albums and baby books. Why do people have photograph albums? (They remind us of things that have happened in the past and of people that we have known.) Explain to the children that you are going to make a group photograph album using the pictures that they have brought in from home. Look at the photographs together and try to decide on a theme such as birthdays, holidays or toys. With the children's help, decide on a layout for the pictures by laying them on the large sheets of paper (leaving space for captions). Let the children talk about what they think is happening in each picture. (The child who the photograph belongs to can explain what is really happening.) Ask the children to help you choose a suitable caption for each photograph. Write it on a piece of white paper, then trim it to size to fit the space in the scrapbook. Mount the photographs and captions in the scrapbook. Make a title page for your album.

If preferred, the children could design and make their own albums using photographs of themselves at different ages or with different family members or friends. Alternatively, the children could take pictures of each other and their local environment, which could then be used to make a group photograph album.

Support
Keep the captions simple, using as many words as possible that the children can already read.

Extension
Use a wider range of words for the captions, and try to introduce more adjectives in them such as, 'Vijay is playing on his new, red slide'.

HOME LINKS
Ask carers and relatives if they have any photographs of themselves as children that they could show to your group.

GROUP SIZE
Four to six
children.

TIMING
Ten to 20 minutes.

WHICH WAY?

Learning objectives
To find about the local environment and how it is arranged; to make and follow simple instructions and read directional words and symbols.

What you need
Several very large bricks of a similar size and shape (plastic building bricks are ideal); paper cut to fit the sides of the bricks (each piece of paper will have one directional word such as left, right and straight on written on it); Blu-Tack.

Preparation
Write out the directional words on individual pieces of paper. You will need at least five copies of each word.

What to do
Ask the group to choose two places in the room, for example, the big chair and the fish tank. Go with the children to the first place – the big chair – taking the plastic bricks, Blu-Tack and papers with the directional words written on them. Explain that you are all going to walk to the fish tank and along the way you are going to leave bricks with labels on them which will explain to other people the direction in which they need to walk. For example, you might need to turn left at the table, and then right at the bookcase, so at both of these locations you would leave a brick on the floor with the appropriate label attached to it. Once you get to the second place that the children named, divide the children into pairs. Ask each pair, one at a time, to choose a place to start. Help one child to leave a trail while the other child looks at a book or does another activity.

When the trail is complete, help the second child to follow it. Hopefully, they should reach the desired place!

HOME LINKS
Encourage carers to use directional words when talking with their children such as, 'let's go upstairs' or 'hang your coat on the peg on the left'.

Support
Rather than writing directional words, draw large arrows. Help the children to decide which way the arrows should point.

Extension
Ask one child to lay out a path with the bricks, then to follow the route, writing down instructions on which way to turn as they go. Encourage the child to remove the blocks and then read out their instructions for a friend to follow.

GROUP SIZE
Four to six children.

TIMING
20 to 30 minutes.

MAKE A STREET SCENE

Learning objectives
To build and construct with a wide range of objects, selecting tools and resources; to read familiar words.

What you need
Pictures of street scenes; empty cardboard boxes (old shoeboxes or cereal boxes are ideal); paints; scissors; glue; white card; drawing materials; palettes; variety of brushes; water pots; large sheet of card; grey paper; small toy cars; play people.

Preparation
If the boxes that you are using are brightly coloured, carefully open them along the seams and fold along the creases in the opposite direction so that they are 'inside out'. Carefully glue the boxes back together along the seams then leave them to dry.

What to do
Show the children the street scenes in the books. Look at the variety of buildings, noticing the different sizes, shapes and colours, and the types of signs that the shops have. Explain to the children that you would like them to each make a model shop or another building, such as a bank or church. Ask each child to decide what building they would like to make, and to think about the type of sign that it might have. Let everyone choose a box, then encourage them to paint the outside of it to make it look like the building that they have chosen. Help the children to make a sign for their building, using the card, to explain what it is.

Place the large sheet of card on a table-top and use this to make the 'street' for a street scene on which to display the buildings. Add a grey strip of paper for the road and let the children add the toy vehicles and play people. Encourage the children, in twos and threes, to use the street for small-world imaginative play. As the children play, you could tape the stories that they invent, or write them down to make a group story-book.

HOME LINKS
Ask carers to look at the names of shops or buildings with their children and to help them read signs on doors and walls when they are out together.

MULTICULTURAL LINKS
Try to find pictures of multicultural shops and buildings, such as a gurdwara or sari shop, which the children could model their buildings on.

Support
Encourage the children to use their early knowledge of writing to make the signs.

Extension
Encourage the children to use dictionaries to check the spelling of any words that they are uncertain of.

LET'S VISIT THE LIBRARY

Learning objectives
To build and construct with a wide range of objects, selecting appropriate resources; to handle books carefully, learn about the uses of a library and have the opportunity to read.

What you need
Table; books (preferably in boxes or on shelves); white card; large square cardboard box; empty cereal box; plain sugar paper; white A4 paper; drawing and writing materials; glue; scissors; recyclable materials such as paper, fabric and plastic cartons.

Preparation
Create a library in your role-play area. Position the table and boxes or shelves of books. Make a computer by covering the two cardboard boxes with plain sugar paper. Add details to make a monitor and keyboard. Place this on the table. Make individual library cards for the children from small rectangles of white card with their names written on.

What to do
Talk about the job of the librarian. Discuss how they keep the library tidy, help readers to find books and 'sign' books in and out. Talk about how people visiting libraries should behave, for example keeping quiet, looking after the books and helping to keep the library tidy. Give each child the library card with their name on it. Explain that when they want to 'borrow' a book, they must give the librarian their library card. Choose one child to be the librarian and let the others browse the shelves and choose a book to borrow. The librarian can use the 'computer' to check whether books are available or on loan.

Now talk about what the children need to do to keep the area tidy. They may suggest placing some bins in the area so that people can throw their rubbish away. Suggest that the children design and make some wastepaper bins. Provide plain paper and pencils and encourage them to think and draw their designs. What resources could they use? Encourage them to choose suitable items from the recyclable materials. The bin designs could be very basic (a tapered cylinder with a bottom), or based on a favourite book character, such as 'Threadbear' (from the story *Threadbear* by Mick Inkpen, Hodder) where rubbish could be put through a hole in Threadbear's tummy. Help the children to collect the resources they need and, if necessary, provide extra support to make the bins.

Support
Encourage the children to plan their bins by drawing diagrams, including pictures of any tools and resources needed.

Extension
Ask the children to write down how they are going to make their bins, sequencing the instructions.

STRATFORD STREET LIBRARY
Membership card

Laura McKenzie   **29/10/1995**

CHAPTER 5

This chapter provides opportunities for children to use a wide range of equipment and materials to develop their physical skills. Activities include a ball-rolling word game to develop co-ordination, a simple dance routine based on the sequences of a story and an action rhyme using picture prompts

Physical development

GROUP SIZE
Any size.

TIMING
Five to ten minutes.

GO TO 'C'

Learning objectives
To move confidently with control; to match letter sounds with the written letter.

What you need
White A4 paper; marker pen; Blu-Tack; large empty room.

Preparation
Write one letter of the alphabet, in lower case and as big as possible, on each sheet of paper.

What to do
Before the activity, stick the sheets of paper with the letters on around the walls of a large, empty room with Blu-Tack. Allow plenty of space between each letter and try to put them where they can be easily read. At the start of the activity, show the letters to the children and read them together. Explain that on a given signal, you would like the children to move around the room. They might like to do this by running, keeping low, taking big steps and so on. Tell them that when you call out a letter, such as, 'Go to 'c'', the children have to find the appropriate letter and stand near it. Once the children have found the correct letter and are standing next to it, ask them to begin moving around the room again. After a short time, call out another letter. Play this for as long as desired. The game can also be extended by asking individual children to be the 'leader' of the game and to choose a way for the others to move as they find each letter.

Support
Keep the number of letters to three or four, and avoid using letters that the children might confuse visually, such as 'b' and 'd' or 'o' and 'c'.

Extension
Stick sheets of paper with upper and lower case letters around the room with Blu-Tack. If you are using both the upper and lower case forms of one letter, make it clear whether you want the children to stand next to the upper or lower case form when you call out the letter. Alternatively, spell out a word, such as c-a-t, then ask the children to find the letters and decide what the word is.

HOME LINKS
Ask carers to help their children to look for and read examples of lower case and upper case letters around the home.

GROUP SIZE
Any size.

TIMING
Five to ten minutes.

STAND ON 'G'

Learning objectives

To move with increasing control and co-ordination showing an awareness of space; to link letters and sounds and initials and encourage letter recognition.

What you need

Large concrete or tarmac area (or large flat area of floor covered with sheets of paper securely taped down); chalk in a variety of bright colours (if you are using paper, use felt-tipped pens or wax crayons instead).

Preparation

If you are using chalk, try each colour on a small area of the concrete or tarmac. Use the colours which are the easiest to see.

What to do

Take the children to the concrete area or paper. Using one of the pieces of chalk, draw a large letter on the floor. Encourage the children to guess what letter you are drawing as you write it and talk about the letter's formation. Give each child a piece of chalk, felt-tipped pen or wax crayon and invite them to draw their own large letters on the ground or paper. Encourage them to look for spaces to write their letters so that they do not overlap each other.

Once everyone has drawn two or three letters, collect the chalk, crayons or felt-tipped pens. Explain to the children that you are going to say a word. As you do this, you would like them to think about the beginning sound of the word – its initial. The children should try to find a letter on the floor that matches the initial of the word. Repeat a few times using different initial letters then invite the children, one at a time, to say a word for the others to find the initial. Help the caller to check that everyone has found the appropriate letter.

HOME LINKS
Ask carers to help their children to try to find 26 objects at home – each beginning with a different letter of the alphabet.

Support

Give each child a sticky label with their name on and ask them to stick the labels onto their T-shirt or jumper. Call out the children's names and ask them to find the appropriate initial, using the labels for reference.

Extension

Call out a short word, such as 'cat' and ask the children to find the letter/sound from the middle of the word, and then from the end of the word.

GROUP SIZE
Four or more children.

TIMING
Five to ten minutes.

WHAT'S THE LETTER, MR TIGER?

Learning objectives
To move confidently and with increasing control; to listen carefully and respond to letter sounds.

What you need
Large empty space.

Preparation
Clear some space if necessary.

What to do
Before the game starts, choose one letter as a group, such as 's', and make sure everyone knows which letter has been chosen. Ask one child to be the tiger and to stand at one end of the space facing away from the other children who should stand at the other end of the space.

Start the game by saying 'Go'. At this signal, the children should ask, 'What's the letter, Mr Tiger?'. To answer the question, the tiger should say a letter of the alphabet. It can be any letter, but the game will last longer if the tiger does not immediately say the letter that the group chose at the beginning of the game! The group then move forward one step (it could be large or small, it does not matter) closer to the tiger. This question and answer sequence continues for as long as the tiger likes.

When the tiger decides to call out the chosen letter, he or she must turn around to face the group and try to tap one of the children on the shoulder. The rest of the group must try to avoid the tiger. The first child to be tapped on the shoulder becomes the next tiger. Continue the game for as long as desired.

Support
Encourage the children to listen carefully to each of the letters spoken, especially if the chosen letter sounds similar to another letter, such as 'm' and 'n' or 'p' and 'b'.

Extension
Use letter combinations such as 'ch' or 'oa'. Encourage the tiger to think of other vowel and consonant combinations to call out during the game.

HOME LINKS
Ask carers to think of five different animals names and to tell them to their children. Encourage them to help their children decide how the words are spelled.

MAKE A WORD

Learning objectives
To move with an increasing awareness of space and others; to make and read simple words, exploring letter combinations.

What you need
Black marker or felt-tipped pen; small pieces of card (playing card size or slightly larger); open space.

Preparation
Write one letter of the alphabet on each card. Make sure there are at least two or three cards per player. You will need duplicates of most of the letters in the alphabet, preferably using the letters most commonly used in English. If you have access to a Scrabble ™ set, the proportion of each of the letters in the game is ideal for this activity.

What to do
Spread the cards out face up in the middle of the open space. Ask the children to walk around the edge of the space then, on a pre-arranged signal, encourage them to walk into the middle of the space and pick up one letter card each. Now call out a number between one and five and ask the children to arrange themselves into groups of the same size.

Once the children are in their groups, ask them to look at the letters that they have picked up. Challenge them to make words containing some or all of the letters. If they have a difficult combination of letters, such as 'v', 'x', 'o', and 'p', change the letters so that they can make at least one word. Ask each group in turn to read out the words that they have made. Put the letters back in the middle of the space and play the game again.

Support
Provide only the more frequently used letters, such as 'a', 'e', 's', 'h' and 't'. Encourage the children only to make up short words containing two, three or four letters.

Extension
Challenge the children to make bigger groups and longer words.

GROUP SIZE
Ten or more children.

TIMING
Five to ten minutes.

ROLL-A-BALL WORDS

Learning objectives
To handle a ball with increasing control; to link letters and sounds, identifying initial sounds.

What you need
A large ball.

Preparation
For each letter of the alphabet, think of as many words as possible beginning with that letter. Try to choose words that are familiar to the children. Make a list of the words for your own reference.

What to do
Sit the children in a circle on the floor with them facing into the centre. Sit yourself in the middle of the circle holding the ball. Explain to the children that you are going to say a letter, and then roll the ball to one child in the circle. The child who catches the ball must say a word that begins with that letter. For example, if you call out 'b', the child could say 'banana', 'boat' or 'biscuit'. Once the child has thought of a word beginning with the letter, they should swap places with you and sit in the middle of the circle with the ball. It is then their turn to say a letter and roll the ball to another person in the circle.

Continue for as long as desired. This activity could also be played in pairs or small groups. One child should call out a letter and then throw a beanbag or ball to another child, who must think of a word that begins with the same letter. The catcher then should then say another letter and throw the ball back to their partner or another person in the group.

Support
Give clues to help the children think of a word if necessary, such as, 'an animal beginning with 'c''.

Extension
Call out a letter and roll the ball to a child at random in the circle. Until you call out a new letter, everyone who catches the ball must think of a word that begins with that same letter, but they must not repeat a word that has already been said.

HOME LINKS
Have a 'sound of the week'. Tell carers what your chosen letter sound is, and ask them to help their children find four or five objects around the home that begin with that sound.

GROUP SIZE
Four to six children.

TIMING
Ten to 15 minutes.

HOME LINKS
Ask carers to give their children the opportunity to write, and see writing, as much as possible at home. Explain how the children have been writing their names using play dough and clay and, if they have play dough or Plasticine at home, encourage them to help their children to spell and write short words such as 'man', 'cup' or 'hat'. Alternatively, provide a recipe for making salt dough which can used instead of play dough or Plasticine.

MULTICULTURAL LINKS

Encourage the children to make names from multicultural stories they know, such as Rama and Sita from the Ramayana (Divali story).

SQUIDGY NAMES

Learning objectives
To handle malleable materials safely and with increasing control; to read letters and names and develop knowledge of letter formation.

What you need
Several sheets of A4 card; scissors; marker pen; play dough or clay; plastic clay tools.

Preparation
Cut each sheet of A4 card into three. Make a name card for each child by writing their first name and family name.

What to do
Give each child in the group their name card. Talk with the children about how their names are written, thinking about the letter formation and order of the letters. You may also want to encourage the children to look at the difference between upper and lower case letters.

Let the children investigate the play dough or clay. Tell them that they are going to make the individual letters in their names using play dough or clay 'sausages'. If necessary, demonstrate how to roll a 'sausage' shape, then invite the children to use their name cards as reference to make the individual letters in their name. Provide help with difficult letters as necessary. As they work, encourage the children to think about the letter formation and the order of the letters in their name. Let them use extra pieces of play dough or clay to decorate their letters, or make patterns using plastic tools.

Invite the children to read their own and each other's names and to look for similarities and differences between spellings. If you have used clay for the activity, leave the letters to dry then let the children paint and varnish them to make a permanent record of their work.

Support
Ask the children to make the letters of their first name only, or just the initial letter of their name. Provide extra support to talk about the letters and their shapes.

Extension
Ask the children to make the letters of their first name and family name, working independently.

APPLES AND PEARS

Learning objectives
To move confidently with an awareness of space, themselves and others; to recognize and read familiar words.

What you need
Four or five sheets of A4 card; marker pen.

Preparation
Write the name of one fruit on each card. Choose fruits that the children are familiar with such as apple, pear or banana.

What to do
Sit the children on the floor in a circle facing inwards. Show them the cards with the names of the fruits on and read them together. Explain that you are going to walk around the circle and give everyone the name of a fruit. Tell the children that they will need to listen very carefully as you would like them to remember the name of fruit that they are given. As you walk around the circle, try to ensure that you have equal numbers of children for each fruit.

Now explain that you are going to hold up one of the fruit cards. When you do this, all of the children with that fruit name must stand up and swap places with another person who also has that fruit name. For example, if you hold up a card with the word 'pear' written on it, all the 'pears' should stand up, look for another 'pear', swap places with them and then sit down. Once everyone has sat down, hold up a different fruit card. Repeat for as long as desired.

Support
Draw pictures of the fruits on the pieces of card rather than writing the names. Give each child a picture of their fruit as a memory aid. Help to keep the circle shape by seating the children on chairs facing into the centre of the circle.

Extension
Increase the number of fruits, and have two or three that begin with the same letter such as 'pear', 'plum' and 'peach'. Alternatively, hold up two fruit cards at once – all the children with those fruit names must stand up and swap places with each other.

PLEASE, MR CROCODILE

Learning objectives

To move confidently with increasing control and co-ordination; to develop knowledge of letters in own name and link sounds to letters.

What you need

Sheets of A4 card; scissors; marker pen; large empty space.

Preparation

Cut each sheet of A4 card into three. Write the name of one animal, such as 'elephant', 'cow' or 'sheep' onto each card. You will need one name card for every child.

What to do

Choose one of the children to be the crocodile and ask them to stand on one side of the empty space – the 'river'. Group the rest of the children on the other side of the space, across the river. Give each child a card with an animal name and help them to read the word on their card.

To begin the game, ask the crocodile to call out a letter. The other children should look at their cards. If their animal has that letter anywhere in its name, they can cross the river to join the crocodile. Repeat until there is only one child left on the opposite side of the river. That child becomes the crocodile.

To make the game more interesting, the children could cross the river moving in the manner of their animal, for example hopping like a frog or waddling like a duck. Alternatively they could make appropriate noises, such as meowing like a cat or barking like a dog!

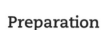

Support

When you give the children their name cards, tell them what the initial letter of their animal is. Explain that the crocodile will call out a letter and if this is the same as the first letter on their card, they can cross the river to join the crocodile.

Extension

Tell the children the name of an animal without giving them a name card. Let the children decide which letters are in each animal's name.

GROUP SIZE
Any size.

TIMING
15 to 20 minutes
(longer if desired).

HOME LINKS
Ask carers to talk with their children about the weather, perhaps when getting dressed or during walks, and to think about how it affects what we do. For example, it is hard to walk in strong wind, and when the weather is cold we want to walk quickly to get warm.

MULTICULTURAL LINKS
Look together at some of the different types of terrain around the world and think about how they may affect the way people move. For example, in a desert the sand would be hot so perhaps you might need to tiptoe, or in a jungle you might have to climb over old tree stumps or jump from tree to tree.

WE CAN'T GET OVER IT

Learning objectives

To move confidently and imaginatively with increasing control and co-ordination and an awareness of space and others; to enjoy books, responding to text by recreating and retelling a story through dance, sequencing the events.

What you need

We're Going on a Bear Hunt by Michael Rosen (Walker Books); a large open space.

Preparation

Read through the book *We're Going on a Bear Hunt* so that you are familiar with the story.

What to do

Read *We're Going on a Bear Hunt* to the children. Talk about the different types of terrain and weather conditions encountered by the children in the book. Encourage the children to think about the feelings of the story characters – were they scared when they saw the bear? Read the story through again, and encourage the children to join in with each repetition.

Ask everyone to find an empty space. Choose one of the terrain from the book, such as the long grass and invite the children to pretend to move through the grass. How would they move? Encourage the children to be as imaginative as possible, and use their whole bodies to explore the space around them. Watch everybody's movements in turn. After a short while, change the focus of the movement to a different terrain. Repeat with all the terrain in the book. Sequence the moves to make a simple dance, which you could set to music if desired.

Support

Focus on just two or three different terrain. Ask the children to sequence them to make a pattern.

Extension

Put the children into small groups of three to six, and let them explore together the different conditions from the story.

THIS IS THE WAY WE...

Learning objectives
To move confidently; to read simple words and pictures and know that words and pictures carry meaning.

What you need
Copy of the song 'Here We Go Round the Mulberry Bush' (from *This Little Puffin...* compiled by Elizabeth Matterson, Puffin Books); pictures cut from magazines showing people doing different things such as riding a bike or brushing their hair.

Preparation
Read the rhyme through and familiarize yourself with the tune.

What to do
Explain to the children that you are going to sing 'Here We Go Round the Mulberry Bush'. Sing the rhyme through and ask the children to join in. Talk about the words and discuss the parts of the rhyme that are repeated. Explain to the children that you are going to change the words of the rhyme, replacing 'here we go round the mulberry bush' with an action such as 'this is the way we brush our hair'. Sing the rhyme through again, this time adding the new words. Encourage the children to pretend to brush their hair at the appropriate part in the rhyme. Now show the group the other pictures that you have collected and talk about what the people in each of the pictures are doing.

Tell the children that you are going to sing the song again, and this time you are going to hold up a picture and you would like them to do the action that goes with that picture. Continue for as long as desired. Once the children are confident with the rhyme, let them take turns to hold up a picture as the others do the actions.

Support
Make sure that the pictures show events and actions that the children are familiar with.

Extension
Ask the children to write down one thing that they do in the morning. Let them take turns to read out what they have written down at the appropriate place in the song.

CHAPTER 6

Creative development

The activities in this chapter encourage children to explore letter shapes and sounds using a variety of resources from newspapers to body parts! There are opportunities to develop skills in using a wide variety of equipment and materials, and to respond imaginatively to what they see, hear and feel. Ideas include making letter print patterns, sequencing events of a story and recognizing sound patterns in words

GROUP SIZE
Four or more children.

TIMING
Five to ten minutes.

HOME LINKS
Provide a copy of the story for the children to read at home. Ask carers to encourage their children to join in with the story and to make the appropriate noises for the characters. The children could also try to think of sound effects for their favourite bedtime stories.

CATS, CARS AND TRAINS

Learning objectives
To listen attentively and explore sounds; to respond to a piece of text and develop understanding about characters.

What you need
Copy of the photocopiable sheet on page 79.

Preparation
Read through the story on the photocopiable sheet to familiarize yourself with the sounds made by each person and object in the story.

What to do
Tell the children that you would like them to listen very carefully as you read to them. Read through the story, using different voices for each character.

When you have finished reading, talk with the children about the story. Ask them if they could think of some sounds that they could use when each of the characters is mentioned. For example, Josh likes trains, so when he is mentioned the children could make a 'wooo, wooo' noise like a train. Help the children to decide on a noise each for Josh and Sarah. Now explain that you are going to read the story again, but this time, when you read out a character's name, you would like the children to make the appropriate noise for that person. Re-read the story encouraging the children to listen carefully and to join in at the appropriate times. Repeat several times, until the children are confident about adding the noises. Extend the activity by asking the children to make their noises quickly, or slower, higher or lower and so on.

Support
If you are trying the activity with a large group, divide the children into smaller groups, each containing the same number of children. Ask each group to listen out for just one name and to make the appropriate noise when they hear that name.

Extension
Ask the children to try to think of noises for the objects mentioned in the story, too. Alternatively, encourage them to work together to create their own story with sound effects.

'C' IS FOR CAT AND CAKE

Learning objectives
To explore shape and form and use suitable tools; to link letters and sounds with objects and identify initials in words.

What you need
Safety scissors for each child; old general interest magazines with plenty of pictures; A4 sugar paper; large wooden letter templates; pencil; glue; glue spreaders.

Preparation
Draw around a template of a commonly-used letter such as 'a', 't' or 's' onto an A4 sheet of sugar paper. Try to make the letter as large as possible on the paper and then cut it out. You will need one letter per child plus a few spares.

What to do
Give each child one of the sugar-paper letters. Make sure that everyone knows what their letter is. Explain to the children that you are going to look through the magazines and find pictures of things that begin with the same letter as the one that they have in front of them. For example, if Hassan was given a 'c' he might be able to find pictures of a car or a cake. Give each child a magazine to look at. Ask the children to tell you when they think they have found something that begins with the same letter as their sugar-paper letter.

Check that the children's objects do have the same initial, then encourage them to cut out their picture and glue it onto their letter.

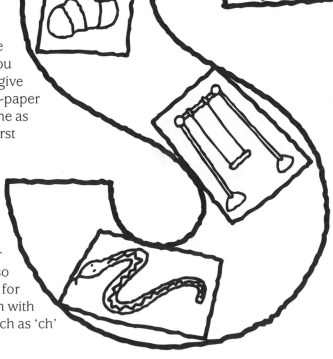

Support
Ask the children to find just three or four pictures to glue onto their letter. You may also want to give each child a sugar-paper letter that is the same as the initial of their first name.

Extension
Encourage the children to find more objects to glue onto their letter. You could also ask them to look for objects that all begin with the same sound, such as 'ch' or 'st'.

CLAP YOUR NAME

Learning objectives

To explore sounds and recognize sound patterns; to say initial, final and short vowel sounds within words.

GROUP SIZE
Any size.

TIMING
Five to ten minutes

What you need

No special equipment needed.

HOME LINKS
Explain the game to carers, and ask them to help their children to think of, and clap, names of different objects such as 'sausages', 'pizza' or 'spaghetti'.

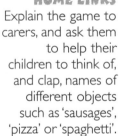

MULTICULTURAL LINKS
Make a list of names from other cultures, such as Aisha, Gita or Rashad. Write each name out on a separate piece of card. Hold the cards up one at a time and ask the children to help you read the name. Once everyone is familiar with the name, try clapping the syllables in it.

What to do

Ask the children to sit in a circle facing into the centre. Explain that they are going to think about sounds, especially the sounds in a name. Tell the children that you are going to say your name, and as you do this, you are going to clap once for each different sound (syllable). For example, 'Mrs Smith' has three claps – two for 'Mrs' and one for 'Smith', a clap for each syllable. Try clapping the names of some of the children in the group. Now ask one child to say their name and clap out each sound. Continue around the circle with each child having a turn at clapping their name. Once everyone has had a turn, let the children try this again, this time saying and clapping their names a little faster so that the claps follow the rhythm of the syllables in speech.

Support

Ask each child to say their name slowly and to clap the sounds at the same time. Encourage the rest of the group to join in, all clapping at the same time and the same speed.

Extension

Rather than simply clapping the sounds in their first name, let the children try clapping the syllables in their family name or surname, or even their address.

ALL DRESSED UP

Learning objectives
To respond in a variety of ways, through the use of art media, to what they see, hear and feel; to understand how pictures can enhance a story, and answer questions about who, where and why.

What you need
Copy of the photocopiable sheet on page 71; paints; paintbrushes; water pots; newspapers; palettes; aprons; white painting paper. Alternatively, the children could draw their pictures on white paper using pencils or crayons, or use pale sugar paper and pastels or charcoal.

Preparation
Familiarize yourself with the story on the photocopiable sheet.

What to do
Read the story to the group. When you have finished reading, invite the children to tell you what they think the characters in the story look like. As a group, choose one character from the story to focus on. Encourage the children to describe the person in as much detail as possible. Are they fat or thin? Tall or short? Do they have dark or blonde hair? How big is their mouth? What colour are their eyes?

Invite the children to paint a picture of this character or to choose another character from the story. As they work, encourage the children to think carefully about all the features of the character. Leave the completed pictures to dry.

Once all the paintings are dry, re-read the story to refresh the children's memories about the characters. Show the individual paintings to the group and ask the children to try to work out who the characters are.

Support
Help the children when they are painting by reminding them of parts of the story that are relevant to the character that they are painting.

Extension
Encourage the children to think about the clothes that the character might wear or to paint the character doing their favourite activity or holding their favourite object.

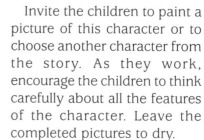

GROUP SIZE
Four to six children.

TIMING
Ten to 15 minutes.

HOME LINKS
Encourage carers to point out different styles of print in magazines, books and newspapers, paying particular attention to the colour, shape and size the letters.

CHOOSE A LETTER

Learning objectives
To explore shape, form and space in two dimensions; to read and say letters and become familiar with different print styles.

What you need
Old magazines and newspapers, ideally containing several different styles of letters; glue; glue spreaders; scissors; sheets of A4 paper.

What to do
Share the magazines and newspapers with the children and look at the different styles of writing. Draw their attention particularly to the adverts, as these usually contain large colourful letters. Ask each child to think of one letter in the alphabet and to tell you what it is. Give everyone a sheet of A4 paper and a magazine. Encourage each child to try to find their chosen letter in their magazine, looking especially at the headings on the adverts. As they find their letters, encourage them to cut them out as best they can and to glue them onto their sheets of paper.

Once each child has cut out approximately ten letters, ask everyone to look at their sheets and try to find two letters that look the same – in size, shape and colour. The children will probably find it quite difficult. Talk about the different styles of printing in books and magazines, and notice how adverts have big, bold, colourful writing to get people's attention. Some of the children may notice that the styles of some of the letters, particularly the 'a' and the 'g' are different.

Use the finished collections of letters to make an alphabet frieze.

Support
Ask the children to find just five letters, and to look just at the larger type of adverts or headings. Encourage them to leave plenty of space around the letters as they cut them out, so that it does not matter if the scissors slip a little.

Extension
Ask the children to cut out more letters. When they have finished their sheets, encourage the children to try to describe the appearance of each letter. Is the letter big? Is it thin? Does it have a loop on it, or an upright?

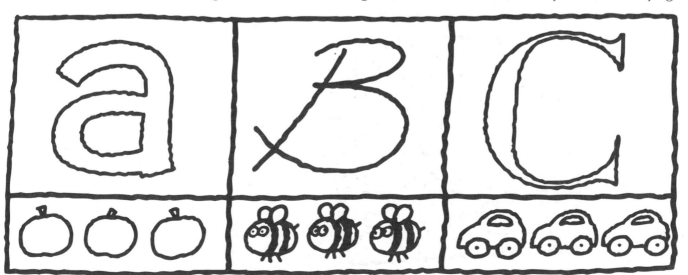

GROUP SIZE
Four to six children.

TIMING
Ten to 20 minutes.

HOME LINKS
Encourage carers to share picture books with their children at home. Ask them to prompt their children to describe what is happening in each picture. Sometimes, the pictures tell more than the text!

PICTURE STORIES

Learning objectives

To express and communicate ideas, thoughts and feelings using a widening range of materials and suitable tools; to understand that books do not need to have words; to develop sequencing skills and show an understanding of the elements of stories.

What you need

Examples of books with few or no words such as *The Snowman* by Raymond Briggs (Puffin Books) or *Rosie's Walk* by Pat Hutchins (Puffin Books); A4 paper; drawing and painting materials.

Preparation

Hide any text in the books by carefully sticking strips of paper over the top with Blu-Tack.

What to do

Explain to the children that you are going to read them a story, but that you are going to read the pictures rather than the writing. 'Read' your chosen book to the children, adding your own observations and comments. For example, if you choose *Rosie's Walk*, you could talk about how the fox follows Rosie, without Rosie noticing. You could tell the children that foxes and hens are normally enemies. You could also discuss the obstacles that Rosie passes safely, but that stop the fox, such as the haycock and the flour mill.

At the end of the book, talk about the sequencing of the pictures and how they told the story. Encourage the children to think of simple stories that they could tell by using pictures, perhaps using just one picture for the 'beginning', one for the 'middle' and one for the 'end'. Ask the children in turn to tell you their story.

Now give everyone some paper and drawing materials, and encourage them to draw their stories. Talk with the children as they work, prompting them to describe things that might happen in their stories that they could add to their pictures.

Display the finished pictures with a brief caption explaining who drew the story and telling a little about each picture.

Support

Ask the children to draw just one picture that tells a story. Encourage them to share their stories with each other.

Extension

Ask the children to make their story longer by drawing perhaps five or six pictures.

GROUP SIZE
Four or more children.

TIMING
Five to ten minutes.

WEATHER SOUNDS

Learning objectives

To use their imagination in music and recognize and make patterns in music; to read and respond to pictures.

What you need

Large sheets of white paper; easel/whiteboard; marker pens.

What to do

Ask the children to think of as many different types of weather as they can. Write each type of weather down on the paper in the form of a list. Next to each weather condition, ask the children to suggest pictures that you could draw to represent each type of weather. For example, you could draw a pair of sun-glasses to represent sun, or an umbrella to represent rain.

Once you have drawn a picture to accompany each weather condition, ask the children to suggest noises that they could make for each picture. For example, for the umbrella, the children could say 'pitter patter, pitter patter', for wind they could make a 'hooo, hooo' noise. Practice each noise two or three times until all the children are familiar and comfortable with the different noises.

Point to the pictures randomly and encourage the children to make the appropriate noises. Try to make patterns by repeating a sequence of three or four pictures several times.

When the children are confident with the activity, let them take turns to point at the pictures, or ask them to think about the volume of their noises. Perhaps 'snow' could be whispered, and 'wind' said very loudly.

Support

Keep the number of symbols to just three or four, and keep the patterns simple using only two or three symbols each time. Encourage the children to predict which symbol they think will be next. Point to each picture slowly to begin with, until the children become confident with the activity.

Extension

Ask the children to think of the severity of the weather. Perhaps they could have a different symbol for torrential rain, or for a light shower.

HOME LINKS
Ask carers to help their children to find three or four objects around the home that they could draw that make a noise such as an alarm clock, doorbell or baby brother! Collect the pictures together and use them with the group to make a sound story about getting up in the mornings.

Four to six children.

Ten to 15 minutes.

Ask carers to encourage their children to look at the different buildings in the local area and to discuss the materials that they are made of. Ask them to make models with their children at home, and to talk about the design, shape and purpose of their structures.

Look at pictures of houses from other cultures such as Jewish flat-topped houses in Israel, houses on stilts or mud huts. Talk about the shapes of the houses and why they have been built that way (availability of local resources, protection and so on). Let the children try to build one of these houses and then write a label about it.

BUILD A HOUSE

Learning objectives
To explore shape, form and space in three dimensions; to respond to a story, and make and read labels using familiar words.

What you need
Small building blocks (such as Lego); story of 'Jack and the Beanstalk' (Traditional); A4 card; scissors; pencils or felt-tipped pens.

Preparation
Cut each sheet of A4 card into three.

What to do
Read the story of 'Jack and the Beanstalk' to the children. Explain that you would like them each to use the building blocks to make a house that either Jack or the giant might have lived in. As the children work, encourage them to use appropriate vocabulary such as 'wall' or 'roof'. Once they have finished their models, give each child a piece of card and help them to write a label to accompany their model which explains what they have done and tells a little bit of the story.

Display the models with the appropriate labels, then encourage the children to read each other's labels. If the children manage this without a problem, try mixing up the labels and the models and then challenge them to put the appropriate label with each house.

Support
Ask the children to write the labels in their own writing, or ask them to tell you what they would like to say and scribe the labels for them.

Extension
Encourage the children to use vocabulary from the book and to talk about the story as they build their houses.

GROUP SIZE
Any size.

TIMING
Ten to 15 minutes
(longer if desired).

THE SNOWMAN

Learning objectives

To use imagination in dance to express and communicate ideas, thoughts and feelings using a widening range of materials; to use knowledge of familiar texts to re-enact the story to others, recounting the main points in sequence.

What you need

A copy of *The Snowman* by Raymond Briggs (Puffin Books); large empty space.

What to do

Read the story of *The Snowman* to the children. Talk about the sequence of the story, and about what happens to the snowman. Ask whether anyone in the group has ever built a snowman. What size and shape was it? Look again at the story and talk with the children about how they think a snowman might move, for example, slowly, carefully and so on.

Take the children to the large empty space. Remind them of the suggestions that they made for how they thought a snowman might move, and then ask them to explore their ideas using as much of the empty space as possible.

Help the children to choose three or four favourite events from the story that involved the snowman, such as when the snowman got dressed, or when he was flying through the sky. Talk with the children about the actions of the snowman during those events and then let the children try to recreate the actions.

Support

Pick just two or three key events in the story, perhaps when the snowman was being built and when he melted at the end of the story. Encourage the children to think about how the snowman would have moved during these events.

Extension

Ask the children to sequence their movements to match the order in which they appear in the book. Encourage them to think about how their whole body would behave, not just their feet.

HOME LINKS
Ask carers to talk with their children about how they use different parts of their bodies for different activities. Alternatively, ask them to help their children look for examples of freezing and defrosting around the home such as in freezers, icicles on guttering and so on.

GROUP SIZE
Four to six children.

TIMING
Five to ten minutes.

HOME LINKS
Give each child a sheet with printed letters on. Ask carers to help their children carefully cut around the letters and make patterns with them. They could also help their children to find words that have the same sound repeated in them such as 'cocoa' and 'tutu'.

PRINTED LETTER PATTERNS

Learning objectives

To explore form and space in two dimensions and use a variety of materials and tools; to read letters and learn about the directionality of print.

What you need

Ready-mixed paints in bright colours; letter-shaped sponges (or potatoes and a knife); shallow trays; paintbrushes; aprons; newspapers; sheets of white A3 paper.

Preparation

Cover a table with the newspapers and lay out the resources. Make an example printing pattern using two letter-shaped sponges, such as 'b', 'e', 'b', 'e'. If you do not have letter-shaped sponges, cut a potato in half and, using a sharp knife, draw an outline of a letter on the cut edge. Cut around the outline to leave the letter standing in relief.

What to do

Show the children your example printing pattern. Explain that you would like the children to make their own printed patterns using their own choice of letters. If necessary, show the children how to dip the sponges in the paint and press the painted part of the sponge onto a sheet of paper. Invite the children to make patterns by printing two letters alternately, then encourage them to try to make a word, such as 'on' or 'at' with their patterns. As they print each letter, ask them to tell you what it is. When they have made a short pattern, invite them to 'read' it to you. When the children are happy with the process using just two letter, move on to use three or four.

Support

Help the children to check that their letters are the correct way up and try to encourage them to print from left to right. Ask the children to print three or four short lines of letter patterns, using just two different letters on each line.

Extension

Encourage the children to try to print their words so that they can be read in different directions such as down the page.

Billy Goats Gruff

In a land faraway, there once lived three goats, called the Billy Goats Gruff. They were brothers.

Through the field where they lived, ran a stream. Beyond it, the grass grew long and lush. It looked so juicy and tasty that the Billy Goats Gruff longed to cross the stream and try it. There was a bridge over the stream, so it should have been easy for them to try the luscious grass. But under the bridge lived a troll. And the troll liked to eat goats!

'I must try that grass,' said Little Billy Goat Gruff, one day. 'Trolls don't scare me.' So he set off over the wooden bridge. Clickety-clack, clickety-clack, went his hooves. He was half-way across when the troll leaped out.

'Ha!' yelled the troll. 'A juicy little goat! I'm going to eat you for my dinner.'

'Please, no!' wailed Little Billy Goat Gruff. 'Here comes my brother, Middle-sized Billy Goat Gruff. He's fatter and juicier than me. You can eat him up.'

'Hmm,' said the troll. 'You're right. You can cross.'

So Little Billy Goat Gruff ran over, as fast as his hooves would go.

Middle-sized Billy Goat Gruff saw his brother munching the long, green grass. 'I must try that, too,' he said. So he set off over the wooden bridge. Clickety-clack, clickety-clack, went his hooves. He was half-way across when the troll leaped out.

'Ha!' yelled the troll. 'A juicy goat! I'm going to eat you for my dinner.'

'Please, no!' wailed Middle-sized Billy Goat Gruff. 'Here comes my brother, Big Billy Goat Gruff. He's fatter and juicier than me. You can eat him up.'

'Hmm,' said the troll. 'You're right. You can cross.'

So Middle-sized Billy Goat Gruff ran over, as fast as his hooves would go.

When Big Billy Goat Gruff saw his brothers munching the long green grass, he said, 'I must try that, too.' So he set off over the wooden bridge. Clickety-clack, clickety-clack, went his hooves. He was half-way across when the troll leaped out.

'Ha!' yelled the troll. 'A big juicy goat! I'm going to eat you for my dinner.'

'Really?' said Big Billy Goat Gruff. 'Well, I think I'll eat you for my dinner!'

He put down his head, and ran at the troll. He tossed him into the air. Up, up went the troll. Down, down he fell. Splash! Straight into the stream.

Big Billy Goat Gruff strolled over the bridge. He smiled at his brothers. They all munched the long, green, juicy grass. And the troll never bothered them again.

© Jillian Harker

Cats, cars and trains

Josh tipped the toys out of the box onto the floor, with a crash.

'What do you want to play with?' he asked Sarah.

'The cars,' said Sarah. 'I'll build a road with the building set.'

'I'll lay out the train set,' said Josh. 'I like playing with that.' Josh began to snap the pieces of track together. He carefully placed the wooden bridge over the road that Sarah had already built. Then he put out the level crossing.

'Can you bring your road round here to the crossing?' Josh asked Sarah.

Josh's cat jumped down from the sofa and walked over to Sarah. It began to purr.

'Watch out,' called Josh, but he was too late. The cat knocked into his bridge, and over it went. He lifted the cat up gently and put it outside, shutting the door firmly.

'Cats shouldn't be on railway tracks,' he said to Sarah, and put the bridge back in place.

Sarah began to push the blue racing car along the road that she had made.

'Vroom, vroom,' she roared.

'Wooo, wooo,' called Josh. He pushed down the barriers of the level crossing. "Careful, there's a train coming,' he warned Sarah. 'Clickety-clack, clickety-clack.'

'Screeeeeech,' said Sarah, slowing her car down so that it stopped just in front of the barrier.

'Miaow,' said the cat, poking her nose round the open window, and jumping down from the sill.

She padded over to Sarah, knocking the blue car from the road. Sarah lifted her up gently and opened the door.

'Cats shouldn't be on roads,' Sarah told her, as she put her outside once more, and closed the door firmly.

She went back to the game. She pushed the car under the bridge. Josh pushed the train over the bridge. Outside, a car pulled up. The door opened and shut with a thud. Then the doorbell rang.

'It's your mum, Sarah,' said Josh's mum, walking into the room. 'She's come to collect you.'

'Have you both had a good time?' asked Sarah's mum.

'It was fun,' answered Josh. 'We've been playing with the car and the train set.'

'But the cat kept joining in!' said Sarah.

'I expect she just wanted to make friends,' Josh's mum told her.

'Miaow,' came a noise from the doorway.

The cat walked across the room, knocking the train from the bridge. It rubbed against Sarah's legs. Sarah picked it up and stroked it.

'Cats can't play with trains and cars,' said Josh. 'But they're great for cuddling, aren't they, Sarah?'

Sarah laughed, and nodded.

'Purrr,' said the cat.

© Jillian Harker

All dressed up

Alice couldn't wait to get to nursery. Today was the day of the big party to celebrate the opening of the new playground, and Mrs Chalmers had told everyone to dress up in their best clothes for it.

Alice had her long fair hair tied in bunches. The ribbons matched the dark blue of her velvet dress. She wore her best, black, shiny sandals and clean, white socks with a lacy frill around the top.

When she opened the door of the nursery, Alice couldn't believe her eyes. There were lots of mums and dads there for the party, but they looked so different to how Alice usually saw them, that it was hard to recognize them.

The lady waving to Mum was Parvati's mum, of course. She usually wore a sari. But the one that she had on today was especially lovely. It was deep green, with a gold pattern stitched on it, and tiny little mirrors sewn into the pattern. Parvati's mum had long, black hair that hung down her back in a thick plait. She wore gold earrings and three gold bangles on her left arm. The bangles shone against her golden brown skin. Alice wished her hair was as long as Parvati's mum's.

Someone tapped Alice on the shoulder. It was Bishram Singh.

'I like your dress, Alice,' he said.

Bishram's dad was standing behind him. He was wearing a long, white tunic and white cotton trousers. On his head he wore a large, white turban, wrapped round and round, so that none of his hair showed. But his long beard looked very black against his white coat. He smiled down at Alice.

'Looks like being a great party,' he said.

Alice wondered where her friend Hatsue was. She couldn't see her anywhere, and she'd told Alice that she would be wearing something special.

'Hi,' said a voice behind Alice. It was Hatsue, but she looked so different! She was wearing the most beautiful blue silk kimono with large, pink flowers all over it. The long sleeves reached almost to the floor. Round Hatsue's waist was a deep sash of bright red silk with white swirls. In her short, black, shiny hair, she wore a huge, pink, silk flower, that matched the ones on the kimono. On her feet, Hatsue wore white socks and pink sandals, with a bar that fitted between two of her toes.

'It's so beautiful!' said Alice.

'I know,' said Hatsue. 'But I brought my dungarees as well.'

'What for?' Alice asked her friend.

'Well,' answered Hatsue, 'You can't wear a kimono on a climbing frame!'

© Jillian Harker

Tongue-twisters

Building bridges

Billy built a big brick bridge
With Ben's blue building blocks,
But Ben built a better brick bridge
With Billy's bigger building blocks.

© Celia Warren

The hamster and the hiccups

Harry's hamster's hibernating,
Hiding in a heap of hay.
Suddenly, the harmless hamster
Wakes up in a horrid way:
Harry's hamster has the hiccups.
Harry hears his hamster and,
'Hold your breath,' yells helpful Harry,
    Hugging him inside his hand.
'Honey helps,' huffs Hamster, humbly.
How he hopes they'll go away!
After hogging half the honey,
Hamster cries, 'Hip-hip-hooray!'
The hiccups halt and happy Hamster
Heads for home and heaps of hay.
'Hush!' says Harry, 'Hamster's having
    Such a healthy holiday.'

© Celia Warren

Alphabet game

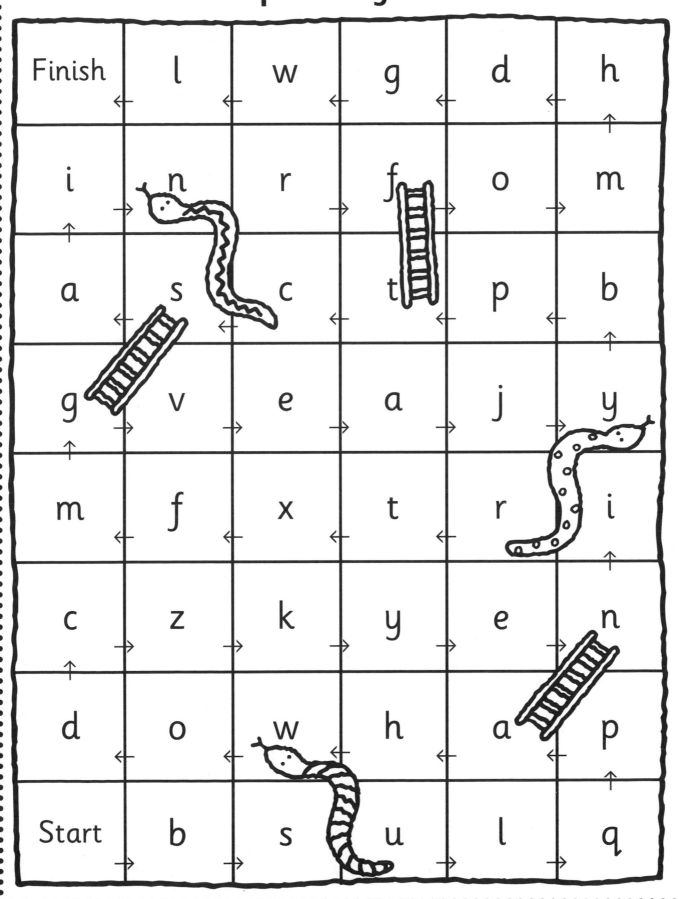

Finish	l	w	g	d	h
i	n	r	f	o	m
a	s	c	t	p	b
g	v	e	a	j	y
m	f	x	t	r	i
c	z	k	y	e	n
d	o	w	h	a	p
Start	b	s	u	l	q

Fall sounds like wall

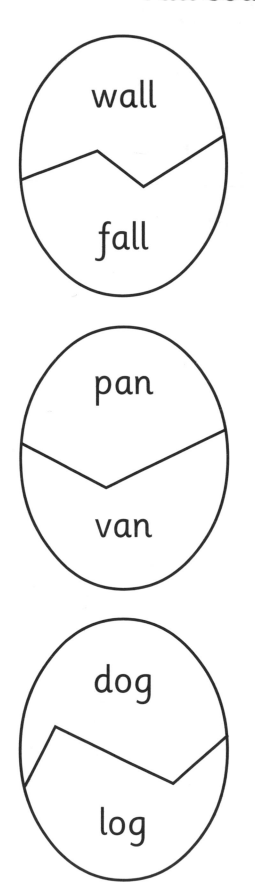

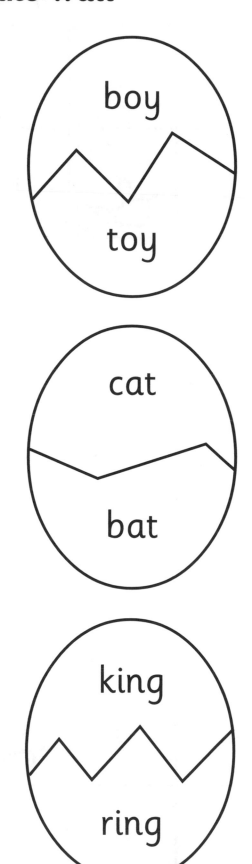

wall

fall

boy

toy

pan

van

cat

bat

dog

log

king

ring

I went shopping (1)

apple

banana

carrot

drum

egg

fish

I went shopping (2)

glove

hat

insect

jacket

key

lemon

milk

nappy

orange

pan

I went shopping (3)

queen

ring

scarf

teddy

umbrella

van

watch

xylophone

yo-yo

zip

Triangle begins with 't'

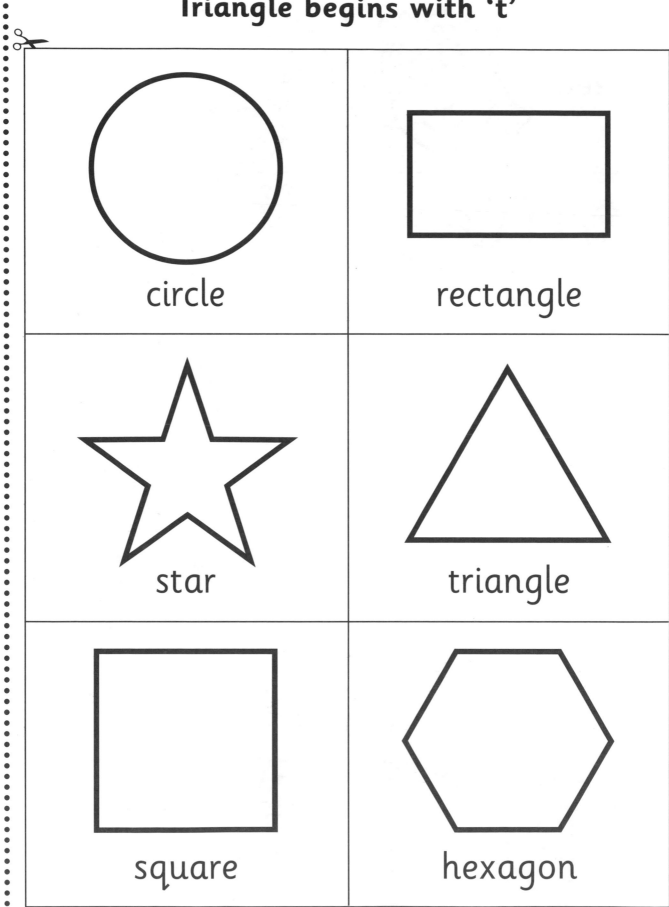

circle

rectangle

star

triangle

square

hexagon

Number plate words

S630 EAT

P794 ARK

M701 AST

H563 AVE

G436 AME

R592 ASH

It's sunny

rain

fog

sun

cloud

hail

lightning

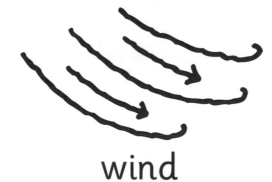

wind

snow